Understanding Today's Students

David A. DeCoster, Phyllis Mable, *Editors*

NEW DIRECTIONS FOR STUDENT SERVICES
URSULA DELWORTH and GARY HANSON, *Editors-in-Chief*

Number 16, December 1981

Paperback sourcebooks in
The Jossey-Bass Higher Education Series

Jossey-Bass Inc., Publishers
San Francisco • Washington • London

Understanding Today's Students
Number 16, December 1981
    David A. DeCoster, Phyllis Mable, *Editors*

New Directions for Student Services Series
Ursula Delworth and Gary R. Hanson, *Editors-in-Chief*

Copyright © 1981 by Jossey-Bass Inc., Publishers
                and
                Jossey-Bass Limited

Copyright under International, Pan American, and Universal Copyright Conventions. All rights reserved. No part of this issue may be reproduced in any form — except for brief quotation (not to exceed 500 words) in a review or professional work — without permission in writing from the publishers.

New Directions for Student Services (publication number USPS 449-070) is published quarterly by Jossey-Bass Inc., Publishers. Second-class postage rates paid at San Francisco, California, and at additional mailing offices.

Correspondence:
Subscriptions, single-issue orders, change of address notices, undelivered copies, and other correspondence should be sent to *New Directions* Subscriptions, Jossey-Bass Inc., Publishers, 433 California Street, San Francisco, California 94104.

Editorial correspondence should be sent to the Editors-in-Chief, Ursula Delworth, University Counseling Service, Iowa Memorial Union, University of Iowa, Iowa City, Iowa 52242 or Gary R. Hanson, Office of the Dean of Students, Student Services Building, Room 101, University of Texas at Austin, Austin, Texas 78712.

Library of Congress Catalogue Card Number LC 80-84303
International Standard Serial Number ISSN 0164-7970
International Standard Book Number ISBN 87589-864-5

Cover art by Willi Baum
Manufactured in the United States of America

Ordering Information

The paperback sourcebooks listed below are published quarterly and can be ordered either by subscription or as single copies.

Subscriptions cost $30.00 per year for institutions, agencies, and libraries. Individuals can subscribe at the special rate of $18.00 per year *if payment is by personal check.* (Note that the full rate of $30.00 applies if payment is by institutional check, even if the subscription is designated for an individual.) Standing orders are accepted.

Single copies are available at $6.95 when payment accompanies order, and *all single-copy orders under $25.00 must include payment.* (California, Washington, D.C., New Jersey, and New York residents please include appropriate sales tax.) For billed orders, cost per copy is $6.95 plus postage and handling. (Prices subject to change without notice.)

To ensure correct and prompt delivery, all orders must give either the *name of an individual* or an *official purchase order number.* Please submit your order as follows:

Subscriptions: specify series and subscription year.
Single Copies: specify sourcebook code and issue number (such as, SS8).

Mail orders for United States and Possessions, Latin America, Canada, Japan, Australia, and New Zealand to:
    Jossey-Bass Inc., Publishers
    433 California Street
    San Francisco, California 94104

Mail orders for all other parts of the world to:
    Jossey-Bass Limited
    28 Banner Street
    London EC1Y 8QE

New Directions for Student Services Series
Ursula Delworth and Gary R. Hanson, *Editors-in-Chief*

SS1   *Evaluating Program Effectiveness,* Gary R. Hanson
SS2   *Training Competent Staff,* Ursula Delworth
SS3   *Reducing the Dropout Rate,* Lee Noel
SS4   *Applying New Developmental Findings,* Lee Knefelkamp, Carole Widick, Clyde A. Parker
SS5   *Consulting on Campus,* M. Kathryn Hamilton, Charles J. Meade
SS6   *Utilizing Futures Research,* Frederick R. Brodzinski
SS7   *Establishing Effective Programs,* Margaret J. Barr, Lou Ann Keating
SS8   *Redesigning Campus Environments,* Lois Huebner
SS9   *Applying Management Techniques,* Cecelia H. Foxley
SS10 *Serving Handicapped Students,* Hazel Z. Sprandel, Marlin R. Schmidt
SS11 *Providing Student Services for the Adult Learner,* Arthur Shriberg

SS12 *Responding to Changes in Financial Aid Programs,* Shirley F. Binder
SS13 *Increasing the Educational Role of Residence Halls,* Gregory S. Blimling, John H. Schuh
SS14 *Facilitating Students' Career Development,* Vincent A. Harren, M. Harry Daniels, Jacqueline N. Buck
SS15 *Education for Student Development,* Jane Fried

Contents

Editors' Notes 1
David A. DeCoster, Phyllis Mable

Part One. Qualitative Analysis

Chapter 1. Academic Experiences and Career Orientations 7
Phyllis Mable, David A. DeCoster
Today's students are determined to succeed in school and, in spite of educational obstacles, they take initiative to prepare for personally satisfying and financially rewarding careers.

Chapter 2. The College Environment 15
Phyllis Mable, David A. DeCoster
Constantly questioning the college environment, students alternately criticize both involvement and apathy. Although disappointed by the ineffectiveness of student governance, they recognize the merits of participating in institutional decision making.

Chapter 3. Personal Values, Attitudes, and Behavior 23
David A. DeCoster, Phyllis Mable
Perhaps the most dramatized and controversial facet of campus life concerns student behaviors that reflect their personal values and ethics. Sexual relationships, drug usage, and academic honesty are issues that receive considerable public attention and scrutiny.

Chapter 4. Interpersonal Relationships 35
David A. DeCoster, Phyllis Mable
College students rely heavily on support from their campus friends, and usually maintain close ties with their parents. However, personal encounters with faculty members and other educators rarely materialize.

Chapter 5. Multicultural Relationships and Pluralistic Life-Styles 49
David A. DeCoster, Phyllis Mable
Students claim to appreciate the educational advantages of living in a pluralistic campus environment, yet minority populations are more tolerated than embraced, more feared than understood.

Chapter 6. Social and Political Issues 57
Phyllis Mable, David A. DeCoster
Most college students pursue personal development as part of the collegiate experience but choose to ignore those social and political issues they perceive as having little bearing on their personal success.

Part Two. Commentary

Chapter 7. The Pains of Growing Up   69
Joseph Katz

Students may move from activism to apathy, but their struggles to grow up are perennial. Helping students in this task is a challenge still not well met.

Chapter 8. Majoring in Self-Interest, Minoring in Apathy: 77
A Challenge for the New Activists
Kathleen M. Downey

Although many postsecondary education institutions reinforce the feelings of students that they are powerless and encourage them to be passive citizens, a new breed of student activist is seeking resources to build sophisticated networks and advocacy organizations on the local, state, and national levels.

Chapter 9. Facilitating Human Development Through   89
Administrative Leadership
Milton E. Wilson

Satisfactions and dissatisfactions of students in postsecondary institutions should challenge administrators to be visionary and assertive in managing the educational enterprise for human development.

Chapter 10. A Developmental Perspective on the Student Voice   99
L. Lee Knefelkamp

This commentary has a dual focus: an analysis of the student voices presented in the main body of the books and an analysis of how students affairs professionals can use developmental theory as a guide for designing campus environments that may facilitate student development.

Chapter 11. Postsecondary Education Futures: Implications,   107
Innovations, and Initiatives
Phyllis Mable, David A. DeCoster

After integrating the messages from students with the wisdom of expert commentaries, the editors postulate change strategies within four broad areas of future reform.

Part Three. Appendixes

Appendix A. Participating Institutions and Campus Coordinators   115

Appendix B. Profile of Characteristics for Student Participants   117

Index   121

Editors' Notes

The professional literature regarding college students is growing rapidly, as behavioral scientists, governmental committees, and institutes for the study of postsecondary education conduct extensive research on individual college campuses. Most of this literature, written for college educators and administrators, is highly quantitative and often based on data collected in relation to a particular theory of human development or educational philosophy.

The public media produce another major source of information regarding college students. Almost always descriptive accounts of student behavior, these reports invariably provide a fragmented, biased, and often unfairly sensationalized view of campus life. Favorite topics include coeducational living, drinking parties, student activism, suicide, and campus crime—narrowly defined issues that are usually presented as isolated segments of the total scope of student life.

The College Student Life Project: Listen to the Students

In 1977 the editors initiated an effort to collect information directly from students currently enrolled at colleges and universities throughout the United States. Our primary objective was to listen to the students and to accurately portray their personal account of the collegiate experience. We wanted to reflect their motivations, goals, and expectations; how they feel about life and today's issues; and in what ways they manifest their values in terms of day-to-day human relationships. The results, we hoped, would provide an honest, straightforward description of college life as perceived and verbalized by students rather than an assessment of their behavior as observed by researchers, psychologists, politicians, reporters, or administrators. We wanted to utilize their thoughts, ideas, and words, to capture the intensity of their emotions and feelings as well as to chronicle their experiences. In this spirit, then, we began what turned out to be four years of data collection, analysis, and writing.

Friends and colleagues at twenty-eight institutions throughout the country expressed interest in the project and graciously agreed to help. (See Appendix A.) Primarily through the dedicated efforts of these individuals, assisted by their local colleagues, 617 college students agreed to participate in small group discussions (typically six students per group) on various topics relating to the six chapters that comprise the first half of this volume. Appendix B provides a complete profile of the participants which was compiled from a brief "Personal Data Form" completed by each student.

The discussions were conducted on the student's own campus and facilitated by a professional educator who tape-recorded the session. Each discussion of a general topical area was scheduled for two hours, and the facilitator was instructed to allow participants to raise specific issues and concerns that were important to them. The facilitator was to keep the dialog moving but not to bias the content or destroy spontaneity by using a directive style or adhering to a restrictive agenda. Students were not asked to respond to our questions but, instead, were provided a forum to communicate their important messages.

Hundreds of hours of taped interaction were transcribed to thousands of manuscript pages. By utilizing the techniques of qualitative research sociologists often employ, the editors identified major themes or trends that emerged from the data. Our general task was to report abstract concepts and objectively identify content areas. We consciously chose to emphasize descriptive comments and direct quotations that exemplified the issues. Our goal was to present a personalized, dynamic account of college student life that would go beyond the cold facts provided by survey research. Thus, we hope the reader will neither attempt to unfairly label and categorize students nor to overgeneralize from their views. We do not intend to blur unique individual human characteristics or minimize the rich diversity that lies within the total population of college students. In the first part of this book, we simply invite you to join us in listening to students.

Commentary and Implications

In the second half of this volume, four outstanding individuals have responded to the student accounts. Joe Katz, State University of New York at Stony Brook; Kathy Downey, National Student Educational Fund; Milt Wilson, Kent State University; and Lee Knefelkamp, University of Maryland, have reviewed the qualitative analysis and utilized their personal experience, individual perspective, and special expertise to provide a comprehensive and provocative commentary section.

Each representing a unique perspective, these four contributors have been nationally recognized for their knowledge and understanding of college student behavior. Their involvement was a rewarding and enriching experience for us, and we are deeply indebted to them for their unselfish dedication to students.

In the last chapter, we attempt to summarize the most poignant aspects of contemporary student life and to link the uniqueness of the qualitative analysis with the wisdom of the expert commentaries. This synthesis produces some requisites for postsecondary education for the future and, particularly, the important contributions that student affairs educators must assume.

David A. DeCoster
Phyllis Mable
Editors

David A. DeCoster is dean of students and associate professor, Department of Educational Psychology and Social Foundations, University of Nebraska, Lincoln.

Phyllis Mable is dean of student affairs and assistant professor of education, Virginia Commonwealth University.

Part One
Qualitative Analysis

Today's students are determined to succeed in school and, in spite of educational obstacles, they take initiative to prepare for personally satisfying and financially rewarding careers.

Academic Experiences and Career Orientations

Phyllis Mable
David A. DeCoster

Meaningful learning can occur as a by-product of academic experiences and career orientation. In the course of schooling, many thoughtful students become more aware of themselves, sure of their coping abilities, and confident about their decisions, both long- and short-range. They accept that their personal development is amenable to initiative, influenced by resolve, and affected by action. Thus, in coming to terms with the educational process, they learn that they are free to shape and direct their own human existence. These students assume their responsibility principally from a sense of determination but also because they enjoy taking initiative and doing high-quality work.

Why Seek a College Education?

Students seek a college education for a variety of reasons and with differing expectations. While many students are expected and even subtly pressured to pursue education beyond high school, they usually approach college with a desire to benefit themselves and a society that stands for prosperity. Certainly, parents can be influential, even forceful, in the students' decisions particularly when they offer economic and emotional supports. On the one hand, society's institutions and educational traditions provide students with a vision of how to meet their own expectations. On the other hand, there is also a keen awareness among students that many parents have "made it" without an education. They sense, however, that both the office and the factory will be revolutionized in the future and that knowledge and skill will be necessary to compete, advance, and in some instances survive. In trying to fathom society and the times, almost every student comes back, with determination, to education's human potential.

Students see education variously as a means to prepare for a career, seek job advancement, relieve boredom, expand horizons, foster independence, and realize personal development. It may surprise some individuals to know that students talk about intellectual stimulation and scholarly activity just as often as they talk about "simply getting through the hassles." Depending on their motives and needs, they talk similarly about the social environment and campus activities. Although they seem only vaguely interested in education's position in the world, students do think seriously about how to become a society of people committed to lifelong learning and productivity. Many share the prevailing belief that a college education is the only way to achieve personal objectives and compete for the better jobs. Several students discuss this idea:

Female: It's accepted in society that you go to college. It's like going to the bathroom; you have to do it.

Female: College was a conscious decision because the job market is the way it is for high school graduates. People are becoming so materialistic and money-oriented that college is a necessity.

Female: My situation is somewhat the same. I found myself at home with nothing to do and not being able to get a job doing what I wanted to do. I wanted a job as a dental technician, and there weren't any jobs available so I decided to take a course in teacher's aide training. It was also a good time to get away from home and do something different and worthwhile. After I got started, I liked it so well that I am majoring in early childhood education.

Male: I came to college because that was the only place to go once I got out of high school. In high school, you're in a basic academic program and not taught in a certain field so you have to go to college to figure out what it is you want to do. And that's the only way to get anywhere nowadays—to have a college education.

Students want an education that enables them to succeed in a society that is committed to both reflection and looking ahead. They want to fit in well, be happy, and do a good job in the things they want to do.

As students talk about their reasons and expectations for seeking a college education, they frequently refer to environmental influences: their hometown, neighborhood, friends, church, influential individuals, family traditions, spouses' encouragement, and media promotion. One student says her motivation for starting back to college was a combination of factors but "Mostly the people around me." Another student asks herself, "Did I have any options? It was as though I had decided, but I really hadn't." Similarly, a male student relates: "My parents, relatives, teachers, and friends of mine in high school all expected me to go to college and I don't think that I ever made a conscious decision."

In today's society, the most widely advanced reason for seeking a college education is the belief that education will open doors. The lesson is described by a student who says, "My college education is making me more significant." Students tell of the need to improve themselves, find gainful employment, remain steadfast and established, and think constantly about their own human realities. One younger student describes the choice as a simplistic dichotomy: "It's be stagnant or go to school." An older student communicates the same idea: "It's the guy standing on the road, instead of the guy standing in the ditch."

Quality of Academic Experience

In a simpler age, the range of courses intended to help students achieve their individual ambitions and total personalities might have been enough to carry students to successful careers. The kinds of conversations that immediately occur as academic experiences are discussed relate to strong uncertainty about major fields of study and career. One student expresses this feeling vividly: "I've seen so many people, like in shock because they're undecided." Concludes another student: "The impression I have is that college is a place to find out what you want to do. And then, it's also a place to learn about what you've already decided you want to do." The central questions the new era of students pose are: "Is it for me?" and "Can I learn the skills necessary?"

Much is left to chance as students struggle to meet the right people and establish confidence in themselves and their ideas. They fear being trapped; they are ambivalent in their searching; and, most frequently, they lack knowledge, information, and decision-making skills. A student describes the pain: "A lot of people feel pigeonholed. And when they come to college it's just like running around in a circle. Because of the job market, you have to become specialized but, once you do and go on to graduate school, what can you do if you decide on something different?" In spite of the ambiguity and uncertainty, students have many hopes. Said one student: "I will do my best. As far as my expectations, I hope to find out what I want to do and do it well." These students' determination to learn, their durability, and their self-reliance will enable them to cope, as they "ask around and figure it out." They quickly learn how to utilize campus resources; they value their ability to think, talk, listen, and do their own research. According to one student, "When you can think, you have the most marketable skill."

Questioned about courses, students agree that the curriculum makes them aware of the complexities of life and expands their view of themselves and the world. While they often complain about distribution requirements, electives, and compulsory course work, they also commend the system of liberal education designed for the individual consumer. In a trade that is lubricated by knowledge and depends on practical affairs and competence, students accept a balance between philosophical and practical education. They argue for social learning in the midst of pressures to perform and bolster the grade point average. In this sense, students are harsh in their judgments of the apparent emphasis on grades, believing that the "mark" is superior to expanding knowledge and intellectual powers in the eyes of the world. Students portray the prevailing spirit:

Female: I don't think about learning anything, really. I think I want to get a good mark in this course. I want to keep my average up. That's all I think about. I have to do this and I have to do that for the course. And that's what I do. It's so stupid—I'm doing all this work for a grade and I'm not even thinking about what I'm learning or even if I'm learning anything.

Male: No one ever asks if you learned anything from a course. They ask what grade did you get in the course. That's just like swallowing the material instead of really thinking about it.

Female: Well, I have to enjoy the classes and I have to enjoy what I'm doing no matter what grades I get. It doesn't bother me as long as I enjoy the class and learn something.

Female: Grades drive me nutty. It's almost like the essence of my whole education. They really do put a lot of pressure on me. I need to get good grades.

Male: I think, for me, grades aren't really that important. They're only important in that I don't want to flunk out and I don't want a low average or anything like that. School is more than just grades. Like there are a lot of other things around campus that students can get involved in. I think that I learn a lot by being involved with things or just talking to another person. These things matter just as much to me as grades.

It is common for students to dream of learning without grades. They envision true involvement and participation in courses, changes in self-concept, and personal discovery. Students view the collegiate environment as making them more aware of personal and world problems, helping them get into groups for close companionship, and providing the opportunity to hear opposing views and become absorbed in deep conversation.

The new student generation is seeking to resolve the issues of knowledge and performance. As one student commented, "My professor lectures to a bunch of people with no heads, and he is supposed to weed people out of majors and careers." Another student talks about "professors who have written books, who don't care about undergraduates, who don't know how to teach, and who are probably known all over the world!" Similarly, students believe that "most professors want you to learn what they teach, what they write, and the things they believe. You have to think in ways that make them happy." A student explains that she knows what the professor wants her to say, but often it is not the way she feels. To a degree, students are disenchanted, but they cannot be characterized as apathetic.

As the new decade swings into full stride, students articulate a "show-me" attitude as perhaps never before displayed. They are looking for evidence that teachers care about students. Many faculty members, they maintain, teach subjects and forget that people require involvement. Listen to their conversation:

Male: Professors just throw work at you, come to class and bull; you have to get the knowledge yourself. Academic freedom is so evasive. Professors have just about all the rights they want, even the right to screw you over!

Female: The classes I enjoy most are the ones that I can really express myself in. I don't like classes where the professor lectures to the class about all this stuff, and a lot of it doesn't even make sense. No interactions. No questions. The professor just talks for the whole period.

Male: I pay a lot of money, and I want to be satisfied with the teachers. I have this one teacher who is ripping off the school and me too. I am paying for him to be there. He says, "You are students and you will regurgitate and give back what I say. Nothing else about you is important to me."

Female: It doesn't really matter what I write on student evaluations of instructors. The deception makes me feel bad. I didn't even fill them out this year.

This unwontedly watchful and volatile student population could turn education into a highly personal, potentially disagreeable, and sharply competitive arena.

Students seem to realize the necessity of listening to lectures and reading books, but they also recognize the role of self-discipline, self-instruction, and personal involvement. Many students pledge rousing and unqualified devotion and support based on their own initiative. This statement by one student is indicative: "Maybe I'm old-fashioned about this, but I think that it is our responsibility to get to know professors and utilize their knowledge. . . . It all boils down to initiative on the student's part because professors are not going to seek us out—they can't. They have all they can do to correct essay exams and papers." Another student asserts, "You have to do it yourself. You have to really seek things. . . . It's up to me to go out and find out what I can do—and that's the way it's going to be when I leave here." Many students believe that they must work for what they get, and that some teachers will go out of their way to assist. More positive students believe there are teachers who care, who have time, and who provide personal attention.

Students often angrily describe insensitive and sometimes callous collegiate environments. Some students feel that they pay for college to receive specified services, and they wonder when the school will deliver something practical. As one student says, "I think a lot of their concerns are with the image of the college—how good their programs look on paper—not the practicality of what you're going to get out of it." Some believe that instruction is a game, as this student vividly describes: "I hate to have to play these games with people. To be successful, you've got to get within the system and beat them at their own games. You have to manipulate the situation around to where you want it. I've been in a lot of systems, and this is really a bullshit game to have to play with adults."

The greatest difficulty students cite with the quality of academic experiences is advising. Students believe that most insight and information comes from other students. One student says that her professor is totally casual about giving advice about "my future . . . my whole life!" "He wouldn't know me from 3,000 other students." Another student accuses the system: "I think that the whole advising process is geared toward the success of the system without any concern for the student whatsoever."

Ultimately, students believe that the reason for a college education is personal fulfillment, and the recognition of this belief may well differentiate the successful institutions of the future.

Career Choices

Setting goals to meet major objectives such as personal satisfaction and financial security is tricky. How can students get good jobs and still know they have found something that will make them happy? It helps, of course, when students recognize trends in the society, such as more women supporting themselves and people becoming more materialistic. Observes one student, "Students today are looking for opportunities, and they are going into fields with money—business, engineering, and the sciences." Another says, "So far as people go, I love dealing with the public, making people happy and satisfied with what I can do. But basically, I'm in it for the money. That's really what makes me want to do the work." Many students seriously doubt that modest life-styles are worth the huge sacrifices: "One thing I have to feel very comfortable about is that I will have enough money to survive and not have to worry where the next dollar is coming from. That's the way I've spent the last ten years of my life, wondering where the next dollar is coming from."

After the initial round, career choices will become more focused. Students choose careers because of real interest, parental inclination, job availability, peer influence, and the reputation of the preparation program. Each individual has a personal story but the basic strategies are simplistic and seem to work well enough. Students perceive that good jobs require good grades, and that job interviews are based on personality. They also agree that it is wise to know a little bit about everything and that decisions made in college are not for the rest of their lives. College, they feel, prepares them for work by expecting quality, emphasizing time organization, and teaching freedom of expression. Explains one student: "I take a risk no matter what I do. Going through college makes me a better person and more knowledgeable—but a degree does not guarantee a job." Another student almost apologetically maintains: "People aren't selfish if they do what they want to do—if they do what is right for them." Another point of view is suggested by this student: "This place is so career-oriented that you are prepared, not necessarily to be a well-rounded, educated person but you are prepared to go into a field and get a job . . . not necessarily to do the job well, but just to get the job."

The major force that sustains students through times of decision making is personal incentive. Struggles to get settled are sustained by competition and courage.

Male: I know I'm one of the best when I do a good job. I know that I'm needed—that they need me. Choosing a career means security in the position, ability to grow in the company, on-the-job training, and opportunity to use intelligence. It also means power, prestige, and promotion.

Male: The things I'm looking at in choosing a career are the location of the position and the kind of atmosphere I'm going to be in. I want a job because of money, location, and how I can fit in with the standards of the company.

Female: I want a job where I can live comfortably, enjoy life, and feel some excitement about the future. So in the next couple of months when I start looking at jobs, I must consider how much leisure will I have, and what commitments I could have to possible job offers.

Female: I know this is different. Mostly right now, I'm just trying to learn as much as possible. I know it's never-ending, but I think I could be happy with just knowing myself and trying to understand what's going on in the world. I could probably be happy doing just about anything.

Female: I think it would be satisfying to know that I might have helped someone, somewhere. That's my motivation for my career and my future.

Male: I feel that if you're going to college, you might as well get into something that is interesting. Even if you can't find a job right away, you can always take another job in something else and wait for an opening. There's no reason for doing something for the rest of your life that you don't want to do and that you don't like.

Students are extremely concerned about having a satisfying life-style, and they want careers that mesh with their personalized, distinctive image. Where they live, how they live, and other priorities such as marriage, children, and avocation are all important variables.

Student's goals range from wanting to "climb the ladder" and be the best to simply wanting to "try out life" and learn from experiences. Women returning to education want something meaningful to do and cannot continue to live through the career of their husbands. Veterans having spent twenty years doing what the "military establishment" wanted them to do unashamedly declare: "the next twenty years are for me." Career choice embodies students' greatest expectations and is viewed as the major variable that will contribute to lifelong personal happiness.

Summary

Student discussions about being in college usually center on their career and financial motivations. They are seeking a better institutional response to their real and personal concerns, and some believe that they can win recognition. Students in college today are expecting opportunities for intellectual, personal, professional, and interpersonal development in their academic experiences and career orientations.

Constantly questioning the college environment, students alternately criticize both involvement and apathy. Although disappointed by the ineffectiveness of student governance, they recognize the merits of participating in institutional decision making.

The College Environment

Phyllis Mable
David A. DeCoster

Students seek a variety of intellectual and personal challenges from the total college environment and have expectations that their education will reflect this kind of balance. In addition to classroom experiences, important elements of college life include the student's living environment, student governance and participation in institutional decision making, part-time work, and campus activities that provide opportunities to invest time and energy in ways that are personally fulfilling. Students point out, for example, that the on-campus living experience is one of the most beneficial aspects of college, that student government organizations help students to shape their own destiny on campus, and that students who have mutual interests profit from involvement in cooperative efforts. Perhaps the most remarkable aspect of students' commentaries was the extent to which they believe college is both an invitation for involvement and a haven for apathy. It is with this sense of ambiguity and inherent contradiction that students describe their living environments, student governments, and extracurricular activities.

Living Environment: Meaningful and Problem Features

The varied living environments students describe reflect the importance of community involvement to the educational process on campus.

Although individual differences, preferences, and aspirations influence students' choices of living environments, in general, they want affiliation, privacy, and freedom. They want to join living environments that reinforce and blend personal development and academic achievement. The following conversation exemplifies some of these needs and desires:

> *Female:* Living at home is difficult because I am still part of my parents' household and they don't realize that college is different from high school. When I was in high school, I didn't study very often. Now, there are time pressures.
>
> *Female:* My first summer at home was hard because my parents were hurt when I did things that went against their values. They ignore the fact that I am a person in my own right.
>
> *Female:* Well, I am living at home and it's not that bad. I would like an apartment and more privacy though, and to be able to do what I want to do. At least, I don't have to worry about food and a place to stay . . . but I would just enjoy myself more if I could live somewhere else.
>
> *Male:* College is a crossover between home and life. I go home for vacations, and it's still my home. Pretty soon, I'll be moving out for good. The crossover bridges the gap between me and the real world.
>
> *Female:* There is so much going on at college. It is hard to live at home and be part of things and it's hard to meet people.
>
> *Female:* I don't make friends with people in my classes. It is not the same as living next door to someone. If I didn't live in a residence hall or have a job, how would I be involved?

What was not explicitly stated may be as important as anything spoken by these students. Achieving a sense of identity, becoming independent, developing meaningful interpersonal relationships, and broadening experiences, sensitivities, and awarenesses are obvious student priorities.

Residence halls currently require little patting on the economic market to flourish. Students appreciate having friends their own age with similar experiences and problems, resident assistants and counselors who help, friendly atmospheres, and manageable expenses. They complain, however, about noise, lack of privacy, isolation, close and crowded quarters, and excessive use of alcohol that often leads to damage and destruction. They realize that experiences are good and bad and that they must learn to achieve in an environment that offers plenty of distractions. One student described her residence hall experience this way: I live in a residence hall and I really enjoy it. It's on the campus and centrally located. The dining hall is across the street. It's nice to live there. It's a lot different from what I'm used to at home. I live with my parents and brother, and it's a completely different type of situation. I have to learn to adjust to new people, different kinds of living conditions. I am never alone."

Many students want to be part of campus and the student body, meet and experience people with different life-styles, and build lasting collegiate friendships. Students praise being exposed to diverse people and ideas. One student explained that she doesn't have to love everyone and yet the exposure is invaluable to human knowledge and understanding. A white student explained how living with a black roommate was a year of learning, companionship, and discovering how life in the inner city differs from life in the suburbs. These students gain lasting friendships and diverse experiences, as well as a high level of satisfaction.

Some students find that residence hall living becomes repetitious after a couple years and they look for other opportunities to assume more responsibility and exercise problem-solving skills in less protected environments. They describe living with parents as continuing membership in the family neighborhood and continuing responsibility with family life, which provides security but limits personal autonomy and self-reliance. Identity problems are raised regarding family, community, and collegiate responsibility. Some students are attracted to fraternity and sorority living in an effort to integrate a study atmosphere, homelike environment, and a collective search for individuality.

In the past, living environments have rarely been described as "home." Some nontraditional students talk about their homes and families:

Female: I'm living at home. I'm married and have two children and I'm thinking about getting help! The problem I have is keeping up the same standards I set for myself before going to college. This shows up in the type of meals I prepare, the cleanliness of the house, and community involvement. Of course, community involvement and church work are cancelled in order to be a student. There is just not enough time to be a full-time wife and mother and be involved with community and church. I have felt pressure from friends who don't understand. They want to know how an hour a month can be a problem. I have had to more or less cut myself off from my other way of life until this degree is finished.

Female: I'm in pretty much the same position. I'm married and have three children. The major problem I have is giving up some of the things I enjoy. I have my own transportation so I don't have to depend on people for rides. Without a car, it's rough—it's a real hassle. My husband helps a lot. We have quick meals. I used to cook roasts; now we have hamburger. He's been real good about it.

Male: Well, I'm married and have four children. I work full-time at night and go to school during the day. I coach baseball during the spring. The wife works, but the children are a big help. I call when I'm getting ready to come home, and supper will be on the table. My little girl makes supper. The wife will sleep during the day, because we work at night.

Thus, the personal lives of students are inextricably tied to academic life, and the impact of the living environment in a changing campus society is more challenging than some educators may imagine.

Student Government: Involvement

An unanswered question may be central to student involvement on campus over the next decade: Will the typical student government's lack of influence, which is internalized by students, be able to become a potent, recognizable force? Most students report that student government organizations are not important in their lives, communities, or studies. Because there is an underlying feeling that student government should be dynamic and effective, students often express bitterness and frustration when discussing campus leadership. As one student puts it, "Student government has no credibility. No one has a positive attitude, and no one believes that senators and committees do anything for students. Senate meetings expound on trivia, self-serving, and wasteful matters." Another student chooses an explanatory perspective: "Most students who know about student government have negative feelings. Student government is only as important as we want to make it. One of the main problems is communication from student government to outside people, and the other problem is lack of student involvement in campus activities."

Although students seem to treasure the idea of a strong, effective student government, they know that senators often run unopposed, elections attract small numbers of voters, meetings bring petty squabbles, leaders like to play politics, and communication to constituencies is always a problem. Thus, it is commonly agreed that student governance lacks meaning, respect, and credibility. This conversation explains what many students are thinking and feeling:

Female: One of the worst things about this campus is the cliques, the groups that people form. My roommate is a senator and it's just disgusting. The senators are supposed to be representing the student body but they are primarily out for their own ego trips. They never get anything done, they do what they want to do, and they seldom report back to the students who elected them.

Female: I rarely hear what is going on with the student senate. Sometimes, I hear because I am in another student organization. If I didn't have a personal contact with two student senators, I wouldn't even know that the senate existed.

Male: Selection of the student body president is a big farce. I try to make it my business to attend senate meetings at least once a month but they are the most ridiculous things. Twelve-thirty at night! The meetings last that long because everyone argues and argues over all the little petty things that really don't make a difference to the average student.

Female: We vote to have senators as representatives, but we never know what they do. . . . They are supposed to represent certain dorms, they make campaign pledges, but nothing is ever accomplished.

Another group of students comments on a similar state of affairs:

Female: I didn't even know the college had such a thing as student government.
Male: I don't take much interest in it myself. I just don't know anything about it. So it doesn't mean much to me.
Female: Me either. I come for an education, and I go home. As far as student government and whatever else goes on, I could care less.
Female: I haven't seen anything that student government has done. I don't even know who is on the student government. I saw a picture that says "Who's Who," and I don't know who half of the people are. It's not publicized enough.
Male: Why aren't these things put to the students? Since I've been here, I have yet to hear a thing about student government.

Students seem alienated and disillusioned with their representation in campus governance. Whether or not such condemnation is justified, a vital segment of the college population expresses a lack of confidence and trust in student leadership. Direct demands for student involvement in institutional decision making may be a declaration of a new understanding required for tomorrow's higher education. Its specifics are almost less important than the sense of the message itself—the need for a student-oriented approach to administering and planning. Students evaluate their expenditure of time, the quality of their involvement, and the effectiveness of their voice in decision making. One group of students evaluates involvement in this characteristic manner:

Male: The administration doesn't listen to the student government. Everything is laid out, and plans are made for ten years in advance.
Male: The problem is that the students can never unite with a strong student opinion and voice. The administration, on the other hand, is always strong.
Female: The main problem is student apathy. Student goverment is not strong enough to do the things that really matter. If the students really got together on an issue, then the administration would have to hear them. Ten years ago, student voices counted because students gave importance to causes, problems, and ideas.
Female: Now, students are competing for grades and jobs, and they don't have time to play student government games. Pressures are real . . . pressures for grades, pressures for graduate school, pressures for job interviews.
Male: The administration should be more concerned with students . . .

what they want and what they think about. They should be available to explain tuition increases, grading policies, faculty promotion and tenure... they should talk with students on a personal level.

A smaller number of students understand that the network for student government officials, residence hall leaders, and student organization presidents forms a talent bank for preserving the political power of students. If students were organized and persistent, they feel, their views and influences could be felt. They also recognize that "the administration" can be persistent and the need for constant student pressure is obvious. Finally, the difficulties of sustaining pressure are equally apparent with a somewhat transient student population who list education and career preparation as first priorities.

Leisure Time

For the most part, students seem to use time not devoted to academic programs freely and naturally even though "goofing-off" is not always explicitly and emphatically identified as their favorite pasttime. While struggling with day-to-day pressures of classes, students focus intently on studies, casually shoot the breeze with people, plan time haphazardly, and support campus activities sparingly. Younger students admit that free time is "fooled away" and usually spent talking with friends. Older students agree that time is already set and spent largely in activities relating to roles as parent, worker, and spouse. Attitudes regarding the amount of free time actually available vary widely, but students generally agree that a great deal of education happens outside the classroom: through employment, living situations, activities, and community functions. As one student explained, "If I hide in my room bookin', then I miss college. If I goof my grades, I could lose the degree." Thus, most students are constantly aware of juggling and balancing their time and experiences.

Younger students spend much time eating and drinking together, playing cards and games, enjoying intensive informal discussions, watching television, reading newspapers, and contemplating the values of more substantial involvement. These collegiate life-styles result from the students' absorbing the culture, as explained in the following discussion:

Male: I am involved in activities, and it has helped me develop in a lot of ways. Relating to people is necessary because that's what I'll be doing for the rest of my life.

Female: That's the way I feel too. When I get more active, my grades improve. If I get involved just a little bit, then I organize my time better. There is a lot of emphasis on grades, and grades really don't say what I am capable of doing. Grades don't tell that much except the specific level of knowledge and information that I have at the time.

Female: Engaging in activities puts what you learn from books into action. I don't get rewarded for participation in activities but getting involved means a lot to me personally.

Another discussion is similar:

Female: I'm not really involved in anything because I work and I'm in nursing, but I'd like to do something. I know a girl who is on the student senate and she can do her homework better because she finds self-fulfillment in outside activities. I've been dying to get into something—I really have. Part of being involved in school is meeting more people and learning to work with others.

Male: Getting involved has taken up a lot of my time but it has also helped me to discipline myself.

Female: Because when you come home you know you have to do something.

Male: That's it. You have to set priorities.

Female: But now you come home from classes and you don't really feel like studying right after you've heard all those people lecture so you make up excuses not to do your work. But when you're involved in activities, you're doing something constructive that is personally meaningful. Then, when you come home, you have your homework to do and that's the next priority because there's no time left to do anything else.

Several factors work against extracurricular involvement. Numerous students must work in order to contend with economics: they fill their leisure time with jobs and studies. Upperclass students often discourage involvement through negative or cynical attitudes. Some students lack the confidence required to join a club or organization while others are simply overwhelmed by the "millions" of things available for leisure and recreation. In the final analysis, however they seem to derive satisfaction from "just sitting around and talking with friends."

Perhaps the most significant change in higher education has been the influx of older students who are attending college part-time. Their presence on campus means taking time away from family, social activities, hobbies, and work. It also suggests that the concept of "lifelong learning" is a reality for many in our society. Older, nontraditional students experience a "constant hassle" within an extremely busy life-style:

Female: When I'm not in school, I am just as busy. There's always something. Something over here has to be cleaned, or I have to go to the bank, grocery store, a Tupperware party. There's always something to do. I hardly have a spare minute. I like to read, and I try to get a book and read a little bit, but I just don't have time.

Male: Married people have it worse. We've got a whole lot more that we actually have to do.

Male: I usually study at night. During the week, depending on how much I have to do, I keep up with studies. I enjoy that. I don't mind it. Then, besides that, I'm working with a band on the weekends, and they have practices and dates. If I don't have to study, then I usually go out and go wild.

Female: I study at night during the week. I do that on weekends, too, but my husband and I try to go to a movie a couple times a month. We play bridge once a month, go to parties, belong to a gourmet club, and go to church on Sunday mornings. The rest of the time I spend carting my kids to movies, skating rinks, bowling alleys . . . whatever, you know.

The mood of the college environment is beginning to reflect the concerns and ambitions of "adult learners." They bring enthusiasm and optimism for education that has its own special quality. They exemplify extraordinary courage and a mature capability to deal with life. It seems inevitable that their dedication, persistence, and no-nonsense attitude will have a sobering influence upon their younger classmates as well as their college-bound children.

Summary

Even students who are dubious about specific aspects of the college environment—the living environment, student governance, participation in institutional decision making, part-time work, campus activities—seem to recognize the significance of involvement. Students clearly value the idea of a commitment to education, and they want educational services that can best meet their goals.

Perhaps the most dramatized and controversial facet of campus life concerns student behaviors that reflect their personal values and ethics. Sexual relationships, drug usage, and academic honesty are issues that receive considerable public attention and scrutiny.

Personal Values, Attitudes, and Behavior

David A. DeCoster
Phyllis Mable

Family, friends, and religion are the major factors that influence the standards and values of college students. Family members, primarily parents, have provided many years of nurturance and are still viewed by many students as the one stable, reliable source of comfort and counsel. This seems especially true for younger students who have only recently moved away from the family environment and who communicate frequently with their parents by telephone and correspondence.

Peer friendships, while viewed as a potent influence, are less stable and more variable than family relationships. Relocating from their hometown to the college environment usually brings dramatic changes in peer relationships. A new set of friends replaces the old, cohesive high school gang, which provides little more than memories. The campus scene, in contrast to high school, often presents students with a more cosmopolitan, pluralistic community and exposure to a broad range of values and lifestyles. In addition, the simple fact that peers are also young adults who, as a group, have not yet solidified a value system contributes to the dynamic nature of friendship patterns. Thus, peers are an immediate source of ideas, experiences, and challenges that significantly affect moral and ethical development, but they are not credited with the same enduring influence as family relationships.

D. A. DeCoster and P. Mable (Eds.), *New Directions for Student Services: Understanding Today's Students,* no. 16. San Francisco: Jossey Bass, 1981.

Finally, religious beliefs seem to be quite varied in terms of their continuing day-to-day impact. Some students cite religious training as the source of good, solid, basic values but believe that at this point in their lives they need to make some independent decisions and choices. Many students are questioning rigid rules, unrealistic directives, and traditional moral values. As one young man described it, "I need to sort out the miscellaneous garbage from the essentials."

Nonetheless, basic religious values emerge in decision-making situations even for individuals who view organized religion as a declining influence in their daily lives. At the same time, a growing number of students describe religion and their personal relationships with God as the central force for daily direction and inspiration. Formal religious services, moments alone in the campus chapel, and private prayer provide strength, determination, and inner peace for these individuals.

Regardless of past experiences and present beliefs, most students agree that they are in a transitional period characterized by change, searching, and continued growth. The following comment captures the sense of inherent excitement in change as well as its tentativeness: "Coming to college has made me become more open to other people and their ideas. In high school, I was constantly surrounded by people with my same beliefs, but here I've experienced different types of people and different values... I used to be very strict, down to the rule, the letter of the law—and I think I'm more open-minded now. That can be good and, maybe, it can tend to be bad."

With this general background, then, students addressed three major issues regarding their behavior in college: drug usage, sexual relationships, and academic honesty.

Drug Usage

Most students agree that the use of alcohol, especially beer, is "a way of life" on campus. Few students abstain and a high percentage drink at least once a week. One student, for example, characterized the successful date as having two major ingredients: "Booze and music." Another commented, "If we consider alcohol to be a drug, then this campus really has a drug problem." The following discussion by a group of midwestern students was indicative:

Male: Using drugs is like trying to escape... I think it would be better to face the problem because drugs and alcohol just temporarily affect your mind. When you come back from your trip, your problem is still going to be there.
Female: Okay, but how many people really consider alcohol to be a drug—and how many people do you know that let it all out after a big test?

They go out and get their mind totaled. I've done it so many times. It's part of college. This whole university is so beer-oriented, so drinking-oriented. I just don't see how you can say, "Okay, I just do it casually on weekends to escape."

Male: Yeah, but you have to consider those people who don't drink at all.

Female: That's a very, very small percent. I'm serious. The whole campus is beer-oriented. . . .

Female: I'm not talking about drinking alone—not at this stage in the game. It might come to that but it's not obvious now. . . . There are people in the dorm who don't need an excuse to drink, and they drink every day just to see how much they can hold. I think this is definitely a problem. Most of us here just drink for the fun of it—socially or not at all.

Male: Well, alcohol, mainly it's just your social event of the school. You always go to the bars and that's where you meet your people. Guys and girls are going to pick up on each other you know. That's your social life—strictly alcohol.

Female: How often do people drink to lose their inhibitions so they can really be something that they're not? Not too often.

Female: I think people just do it for fun. I don't think too many kids at our age are alcoholics who have real big problems where they need an escape. We think school's a big problem but people say this is the easiest thing we're going to do.

Female: I agree that the majority of the kids drink just because it's fun, not to escape or lose their inhibitions.

Thus, while some students use alcohol as a means to combat academic pressures, reduce anxiety, or escape from stress, the overwhelming factor regarding drinking behavior is simply that it is in vogue—it is the "in thing to do." Drinking is fun, it is relaxing, and it has widespread social acceptance within the student culture.

The general attitude toward marijuana is one of casual acceptance. Although not as predominant as alcohol use, marijuana is accessible and smoking pot is considered rather routine. According to one student, "Right now it's more public. If you go back ten years or so people seemed to plan private or closed parties—'let's get together and smoke some grass this weekend'. Now, it's more publicized. You walk down the hall and someone says, 'Hey, you got some? You want to get high? Want to smoke? Let's get high'. You know how it is—it's more open. That's all there is to it."

Most students are familiar with marijuana through either past experiences or current experimentation. Perhaps not surprisingly, then, smoking grass has lost much of its romantic, exotic, or counterculture attractiveness with contemporary students. Many students, for example, talked about their personal drug use and abuse in the past tense while, at the same time, described the current behavior of other students on campus. As one woman explains:

> I used to be a very ardent drug user for about five years. I was into a wide variety. To this day, I have no regrets about my past. I choose to laugh at it. I wouldn't be me if I hadn't gone through that stage first . . . I went cold turkey at the beginning of my senior year in high school. My friends hung by me—they couldn't understand what was going on because it was like two different stories; a flip of the coin. They supported me and when I got here, well, it's been kind of tough, especially with marijuana because it's so socially accepted. On many occasions, I'll have a beer but I won't have a bong. Actually it's really kind of hard for me to explain, but I feel like once I go back and take a hit I'll be right into the swing of things all over again. I still come in, like you know everybody on the floor parties high, and I'll sit right down and rap with them. I don't have any inhibitions about it but I'll leave drugs to my past. I won't get back into that . . . it chains me down.

For most students, the change in behavior is less dramatic but a cyclical pattern of drug use, especially with marijuana, is apparent. A growing number of young adults are introduced to drugs long before their college years, they have experienced a stage of fascination or almost compulsive indulgence, and now they feel the security of a mature perspective. These students get high occasionally but their drug-related behavior is not influenced by peer pressure or a desire to feel accepted. They have "been there" and they feel comfortable with moderate levels of drug use. Other students, of course, are exposed to drugs for the first time as college freshmen and, thus, may not achieve the same level of maturity until their junior or senior year.

Male: I have found that a lot of people drink and smoke pot for social acceptance. It's the in thing. I've seen it among all my friends. During my first year, there were sixty-five freshmen on our dorm floor. There were water fights, shampoo battles, pillow fights—drinking all the time. Now we have very little drinking and water battles are nonexistent. The seniors who do drink, don't advertise it. It's no longer the in thing to drink or smoke, and as a result the number of people who drink excessively are very few. And the people who drink are doing it because they enjoy it.

Female: A lot of it, I think is that it's the first time these people have been away from mother and dad. They just like the idea that they can stay out all night and drink all they want. A lot of them say, "Oh if my parents could see me now—if they could see what I'm doing."

Female: A girl told me to be careful before I even came to college. She said that you can always tell a freshman girl—she's the one being dragged in by her date because she's so drunk. I think you're really right. I think it's just the fact that you get away from parents. One of the first things there is to do when your parents aren't around is to drink a good deal.

Thus, while excessive or inappropriate drug use by some individuals is apparent, immature or obnoxious behavior is often viewed by experienced students as a "stage" that will probably have to be tolerated. "Getting wasted" on a regular basis or being "constantly fucked up," however, is generally recognized as unhealthy behavior expressed by a novice, immature, or troubled student.

At any rate, whether the causal factor is peer pressure, curiosity, social acceptance, or freedom from parental direction, the accessibility and routine use of various drugs on campus makes some experimentation for inexperienced freshmen probable:

Female: It was hard to get a hold of drugs before but here I can knock on almost any door and at least be lead to the right place. I'm ashamed to say that but I know it's true from experience.

Female: I think mushrooms* are prevalent on campus. People talk about shrooming and alcohol—they are the main things. And people smoke marijuana excessively.

Drugs other than alcohol and marijuana do not enjoy much popularity and appear to be used sparingly by only a small percent of the college population. Uppers (stimulants, especially amphetamine derivatives) and downers (depressants, such as barbituates and tranquilizers) are still used by some students primarily in relation to late-night or all-night study sessions. The traditional use of coffee and "across-the-counter" pills containing caffein, however, are the typical methods of staying awake. Heroin, morphine, and hallucinogens such as LSD are generally classified as "hard drugs" by students and, while their presence on campus is sometimes rumored, the actual use of these drugs is minimal. Health dangers, legal consequences, high cost, and low accessibility are all variables cited for their low profile on the college scene. Even "Angel Dust" or "PCP" (phencyclidin), which has received so much media attention in recent years, was rarely mentioned.

Sexual Relationships

Sexual relationships on campus generally reflect permissiveness in terms of actual behavior as well as personal attitudes. For some individuals,

---

*Mushrooms grown in Mexico (containing the drug psilocybin) are eaten to achieve a hallucinogenic effect similar to that obtained from LSD. We found this practice popular only on this particular campus.

women and men alike, sexual intercourse is an expectation even on the first date. Thus, asking for a date has become synonymous with asking a person to go to bed. For most students, however, there is a clear distinction between "having sex" for purely physical and sensual reasons and "making love" within the context of a caring relationship. The following comments of two women at a southern institution capture some of the prevailing feelings:

> *Female:* As far as sexuality is concerned, it's really impressive how much things change as you get older. In junior high school and high school, your parents have a lot to do with how you feel about sex. My mother told me that she didn't want any grandchildren and my father told me that I had better not come home pregnant. Now, as I get older, I find that it's more of a total thing with me. It's what I want. And if I find somebody that I want to get involved with—if I really trust him and if I find that it's what the two of us want to do—the decision has nothing to do with what everybody else is doing or not doing or that mom and dad said not to do it. Now I've reached the point where, if I want to get involved with somebody, it's just between me and the other person.
>
> *Female:* I think what I value most about sexuality is that it's a good outlet to really create an expression without my having to put that creativeness into words and language. I can directly create how I feel with my body and specifically, and I really like that feeling. I like being able to share that feeling with someone. . . . But I don't like what our generation is doing with sexual morals. I'm not comfortable with the ideas expressed by people of our generation—let's go out tonight, let's get it on, you know, that kind of thing. I'm not that kind of person. I have to build a relationship before something like that would happen.

Another discussion among students at a small western institution provides some additional insight regarding attitudes toward casual sex:

> *Male:* As far as sex goes, I think it's taking on a connotation of irresponsibility. Some freshman girls come here and get into bed, get sex, especially girls that come in and throw themselves down. . . . It's something I think a lot of girls use to get what they think they want and it doesn't work. There should be an understanding about love—people don't know. I can personally say that I love my family and I question whether I love any girl. I don't know that I have—I pretend a lot as far as sex goes.
>
> *Female:* You were talking about freshman girls coming in and throwing themselves down. Why?
>
> *Male:* Because they think they've got a friend when they put out, then they're going to. . . .
>
> *Female:* Get something in return? . . . Do you think it's the need for

acceptance? Do you think it's trying out the adult world? . . . What's the motivation?

Male: It's first experience; second, it could be a rebellion against parents or society; third, it's the sensation. . . .

Female: I think freshmen really want to be accepted and cared for because it's scary, very scary—it's hard at first. Who's going to be my friend? Am I going to have any friends? Am I going to sit in my room every Friday and Saturday night? I see people doing those things in trying to be accepted and trying to find out what love is about. But they're putting the cart before the horse and I think it should be the other way around, the horse being love. . . .

Male: I'll tell you the difference—genital sex is pumping, and sex, well, it's making love. Genital sex is one set of organs . . . that's just a hump.

Female: It's kind of like Wednesday, the hump day isn't it? But how many people have been held so tight by someone they love and that's all. And felt so secure by the person holding you that you're totally satisfied, physically and emotionally. . . .

Female: I think men are looking for that too because I know a lot of guys are scared of women because they're afraid that they have to perform. One guy very honestly said to me, "You know, you girls let us know on the first date. I mean, we think we're supposed to kiss you, put our arm around you, and ask you to go to bed on the first date. We're real scared about it." Now that may be a generalization, but I have had a tendency to think all guys want your body on the first date, and I know that's wrong and I have to change my thinking.

Men confirmed that the permissive atmosphere, playboy stereotypes, and particularly the expectations and direct comments from women provide a source of pressure to make sexual advances—to perform.

Male: I've dated girls and if I didn't spend the night with them after three or four dates, you know, their feelings were hurt. . . .

Male: I had a girl ask me after I had dated her for about four or five weeks without going beyond kissing—she wanted to know if I was normal. . . . When it gets so loose that your date thinks there's something wrong with you or that they're inadequate in some way, that really shows how immature the whole situation is getting. You really get in trouble when you put sex ahead of anything else without getting to know the person.

With a similar sense of confusion, men report a growing number of occasions when women ask them for dates or assume a more aggressive role regarding sexual encounters. There were additional indications that the double standard continues to weaken. College men, for example, maintain that they do not expect or prefer to marry virgins, and women often recognize and consciously fulfill their sexual needs. There continues to be the feeling among women, however, that negative reputations based upon sexual activity are prevalent and generally work to their disadvantage. Some men were surprised to learn that women "compare notes" and, therefore, the males develop reputations as well.

At the same time, women expressed frustration with men who have preconceived sexual expectations, assume that they are somehow entitled to sex as part of a date, and especially those who grab, paw, or use physical force to make advances. Phony lines and sweet talk, attempts to make a woman who refuses them feel guilty or prudish, and the apparent dating popularity of women who are more sexually active were identified as tiresome male behavioral patterns. One woman tersely commented, "In some circles, if you don't put out—you don't go out." Others expressed similar thoughts:

Female: I think a lot of fraternity guys just try to put notches on their frat paddle or whatever they have. They try to get a string of wins. I think that how many girls they get on a weekend is like how many cases they drink—some kind of status symbol.

Female: Kind of a macho male thinks you're hot to trot. . . .

Female: Sex can be such a hassle. I don't think sex is bad—it's only natural when you feel for someone and you have an intimate relationship. But when you can't go out on a decent date without being propositioned—that makes me feel real yucky. There's too much emphasis on it, and people try to attach making love to just an "easy screw." I think that is cheap, and people don't understand the difference between a one-night stand and a relationship where there's trust and love and honesty.

Finally, through the general permissiveness with its struggles and pressures, both men and women visualize an eventual relationship that they describe in somewhat traditional terms. The desires for interpersonal security, stability, and commitment were identified as important elements of a lasting, loving relationship within the context of a family unit.

Academic Honesty

If there is one area in which students are in total agreement, it is the observation that academic dishonesty on campus is widespread. Perhaps more surprisingly, much of the cheating is done quite openly, without shame or guilt and with little fear of repercussions. The predominant attitude toward academic dishonesty was captured in the following discussion:

Male: We're talking about large percentages. You're always going to have cheaters in class but as far as I'm concerned the guys in my classes—

they cheat and they just laugh in the back of the room. The teachers know about it, and you go up and tell the teacher that the people back there are cheating, and they don't even act like they care—and you're fighting for a grade just to make it.

Female: Yeah, I mean you can rationalize it by saying that they're going to lose out in the long run but to have a teacher turn around and say, "Tough, I can't do anything about it. . . ."

Female: If you're going to go up there and risk a lot of peer agitation—going up there and saying, "Hey, they're cheating back there" . . . a lot of your peers will look down at you. Maybe it isn't a big thing to have people who are cheating looking down. . . .

Female: The same with term papers, you know, they're floating around all over the place, too.

Female: If they can't take the time to write it themselves, they really don't deserve to get the grade on it anyway.

Female: They do, they end up getting the grade, and they end up getting a better score than you. You stay up two nights working on it, and they went down and paid about fifteen dollars for a term paper, and maybe they just erase the name and type in their name. They end up getting an "A" and you end up getting a "C." There's no way you can qualm about that because that's just the way it is.

Male: Term papers are rather hard to check on cheating. You can prevent people from cheating on tests—nobody can tell me you can't. If the teacher would write up four or five different series of tests, all having the same questions, all you have to do is rotate the questions or use a different series of tests each semester—do that instead of using the same test over and over again. That can prevent it, plus having the teachers watch the class when they take a test. Most of the time, teachers don't even care. They just walk out.

Female: Walk out, that just encourages cheating. . . . Students feel if he doesn't care enough to watch over what we're doing then, you know—forget it. If he doesn't care that much, I'm just going to get a better grade if I can.

Male: In one tech class I took . . . there were quite a few people in there who were cheating, and we all knew about it. There were about eight or nine of them who would just sit in the back of the room and cheat. It was hard enough to make a grade in the class as it was, well, the teacher was confronted with it. A bunch of guys went up and told him that there was cheating going on and he was using the same old tests that he used last year. Well, of course he didn't say too much. He said, "Yeah, well, okay, I know what's going on."

Female: And then forgets about it.

Male: Right . . . all he would do was give you a quiz every day instead of lecturing and when he did get up for the lecture, he had no structure to his lecture. You didn't know what to take notes on. His tests would have nothing to do with what he lectured on, and his attitude was just really, "Well, I don't care." So finally I just got smart, and I started getting tests, saying, "Well, if that's the way it's going to be, you know, I'm going to get tests, too."

Perhaps the major reason, or rationalization, offered by students for the high incidence of academic dishonesty was the "message" they receive from many instructors. Poor teaching, arbitrary grading systems, and the general lack of interest on the part of faculty members to prevent dishonesty are often interpreted to mean that "cheating is all right as long as you are not too obvious—as long as you do not get caught." A distressed woman describes one of her courses this way:

> I had an instructor last year who sold his notes at the beginning of the semester—sold his notes for a dollar apiece. We bought the notes and went through them and he got up and put the same notes up on the projector and read through them . . . and then we'd have a quiz every other day. I remember a girl raised her hand about the second day to ask a question, and he said that he had no time for questions—that he was on a tight schedule and that this is every day. Every day he's going to lecture on certain things on the outline, and if you had any questions, you should make an appointment to talk to him, which I think was full of shit, really. I mean, if you can't even ask a question when you have something on your mind. I don't have time to run down and make an appointment. I feel like they ought to take the material slower and if you have a question, answer it.

It is this type of uncaring and detached instruction that contributes to student beliefs that college is more a matter of "getting through" than a process of learning. Cheating, they maintain, is often a direct extension of the way in which professors run their classes. Such concerns seem to fall into three categories.

First, when a teacher makes it easy to cheat or does not confront obvious dishonesty, students assume "anything goes" as the norm for that class. Typical teacher behavior that contributes to this attitude includes administering the same tests semester after semester, leaving the room during a test rather than actively monitoring the examinations, and returning written assignments without constructive feedback to the student— without evidence that the paper was reviewed carefully or even read completely. One student illustrated this latter concern by revealing that she had copied an "A" paper from the previous semester to raise her average and received a "C" on it from the same instructor.

Second, although examples are less frequent, direct knowledge of a teacher's dishonesty seemed to be evidence of an uncaring system. Obvious favoritism for athletes was most often cited. One woman, for example, was offered a job by the Athletic Department to write papers for football players. Another student found that he had flunked a course even though he had a considerably higher semester average than an athlete who had received a passing grade. In his words, "grades are averaged kind of funny when it comes to star athletes." And a paid academic tutor for athletes shared his direct knowledge of situations in which athletes have easy accessibility to tests and term papers and of professors who complain about continuing to do "academic favors" for players who lose football games. Sexual favoritism was mentioned as a concern but such incidents were much less common and less explicit. The typical circumstances involved a male instructor providing some sort of special help or advantage for a female student.

Finally, many students simply blame their instructors for various pressures that make academic success difficult. Thus, extremely difficult tests, trick questions, unrealistic expectations, and a large quantity of assignments often frustrate a busy student who is trying hard to succeed. Unfortunately, such circumstances are often used to rationalize or condone dishonest behavior.

In all, these conditions lead to a mixture of anger, embarrassment, and resentment among students. The following discussion captures some of the incongruity and desperation:

Female: The only person who is rewarded is the best . . . they never take the honest person, they take the best person. . . .
Male: The thing that disturbs me is that somewhere along the line we've lost the rules.
Female: From our youth we have been taught to be honest, that we should think of other people. Yet when we get into college and start interacting with society, the family rule no longer holds up. We start competing and become selfish.

For some students, the pressure of college competition is compounded by parental pressure to succeed. And peer pressure can ostracize a person who reports dishonesty to authorities. Thus, it is common for students to struggle in clarifying their personal positions regarding cheating and in identifying situations that they are willing to confront. A "secondary code" for academic honesty defines various degrees of cheating. Cheating in a class that is graded on the curve, for example, directly hurts other students and is less acceptable than dishonesty in other courses. Similar reasoning declares using crib notes as a lesser degree of cheating than copying from someone's paper. As one student put it: "I think we should differentiate between cheating and corresponding cheating where you know the guy beside you and you're in cohoots together. I don't like the idea of staring at someone's paper who you don't even know. That's not my style. Getting in cohoots with a buddy is different."

Directly and purposely harming another student's chance to compete fairly is most objectionable. Thus, to sabotage a chemistry experiment or destroy another student's notebook is rarely condoned. In contrast, students who consistently skip class and borrow notes from classmates to keep up are disliked but tolerated. A male student who has several female students taking notes for him is known as an "academic pimp." Although it made her mad and disgusted, one woman confessed: "When a good-looking guy asks to borrow your notes, you just can't say no and walk away."

The general agreement among students was that they would be more likely to confront the individual than to report cheating to the instructor or other authorities. Going to the teacher presents a risk with classmates and is generally not viewed as effective anyway. Directly confronting individuals, however, presents the potential of "helping" them and preventing further episodes. Some students said that they would talk to friends and acquaintances about cheating offenses but believed that confronting strangers involved too much time, hassle, and emotional energy.

Summary

Students attribute their moral development to family interactions, peer friendships, and basic values founded in religious training. Their personal behavior and attitudes toward campus life, however, reveal an atmosphere of sexual permissiveness, casual acceptance of marijuana, and an almost universal preoccupation with drinking alcoholic beverages—especially beer. Perhaps of greatest significance and concern was the open acknowledgment that academic dishonesty in college is so widespread that many students consider cheating a necessity in order to remain academically competitive. These features of contemporary college life-styles create internal turmoil, frustration, interpersonal conflicts, and a sense of uncomfortable selfishness and hedonism among some students. Thus, they discussed negative consequences derived from their generalized version of situational ethics as well as some positive, healthy attitudes that accompany an atmosphere that is free, open, and self-reliant.

College students rely heavily on support from their campus friends, and usually maintain close ties with their parents. But personal encounters with faculty members and other educators rarely materialize.

Interpersonal Relationships

David A. DeCoster
Phyllis Mable

Most educators will acknowledge the important contributions of meaningful interpersonal relationships to the growth and development of college students. It is becoming more obvious that the learning and maturation process involves a combination of all the experiences that impinge upon a student's life during the college years. Thus, a "college education" is composed of an array of learning opportunities that transcend the world of classes, credit hours, textbooks, examinations, and grades associated with the formal curriculum. In this context, significant and meaningful relationships with others are recognized as a powerful developmental influence. The following pages of this chapter will describe student relationships with peers, parents, and older adults within the campus community—primarily faculty members.

Peer Relationships

The transition from high school and hometown friendship patterns to the new collegiate environment is often viewed as a difficult, and sometimes traumatic, experience for young adults. Students can feel homesick, isolated, or alienated in their new world. One freshman woman expresses the sense of loss this way: "I haven't really found that I have friends here—I haven't found anyone like my friends at home. We were

D. A. DeCoster and P. Mable (Eds.), *New Directions for Student Services: Understanding Today's Students,* no. 16. San Francisco: Jossey Bass, 1981.

really tight and when those of us who went to college get together, we share our experiences. But something is different on campus. I need a friend up here just like the ones at home, and I'm trying to find one. You can make a lot of acquaintances in college—I know twice as many people as I do in the city where I lived for nine years. But I don't really know them and there are not as many people I can call when I really need help."

Tragically, the dynamics captured in the following discussion can contribute to desperate feeling that combines the elements of helplessness, loneliness, and fear of failure:

Female: Well, you're down here for you, and you know that you're the only one who can get the job done. You can get help along the way, but you have to be motivated to get through college and you have to set goals by yourself.

Male: The feelings are usually a little bit more intense when you get to college. In high school, people think that when they get to college everything will straighten out and they will know exactly what they want to do. . . . Some people, though, are still thinking: "I'm here but I still don't know what the heck I'm going to do." I don't want to generalize too much, but some people withdraw and lose confidence because they feel like they spent eighteen years and now they're here, and things still haven't fallen into place.

Female: Right, they're trying to prepare themselves and, like you said, it's kind of late to be trying to get themselves together. You should be together and know what you're going to do.

Male: Which is usually one of the reasons for the high suicide rate among college students.

Female: How depressing.

Male: Like I said, I tend to analyze stuff like this and it's true. Now, personally I don't mind saying it because I feel perfectly fine, and I know what I'm going to do. If there's somebody else here who's not too sure, I'm not going to say anything—they might go out and hang themselves or something.

Female: I have never found myself more depressed than I have since I came to this school, and I don't know if this has anything to do with the topic or not, but I don't know what it is.

Female: Do friends help you?

Female: Friends?

Female: Do you rely on your friends?

Female: I think I probably rely on them too much which is maybe why I . . . I don't really know how to explain it. It's like I'm supposed to know what I'm doing right now, and I know what I want to do but I don't think there's any way that I'll be able to do it. So you get depressed and you think, "What else can you know? What else could be my major? What else can I do? Why don't I just quit school and go home and get a job?"

For some students, then, college life, particularly the first year, can be a somewhat lonely, insecure, and threatening experience. Most students, however, find their introduction to the campus community to be an exciting, challenging transitional period. Family mobility and the routine changes from grade school to junior high to high school have prepared many students to handle such circumstances with relative ease. Meeting new people and losing intimate contact with past friends has become a part of life. Many of these same students reflect on their high school cliques and narrow stereotypes with considerable insight and remorse:

Female: There were some people who wanted to be in groups, and then there were some who got put into groups by others.
Male: Yeah, you fell into a certain group whether you wanted to or not. . . .
Female: You may not have thought that you were a certain group, but other people thought you were and they classified you. It determined who your friends were and who you liked.

Another group of students also exemplified the confining, limiting nature of high school relationships:

Female: My friends were from the cheerleading squad in high school. . . . Everyone expected us to be friends, so we were friends. When you meet someone in college, you don't know what they were like—they could have been the biggest losers in the world! But you don't know that, and they come out being great. It's nice to know a person and not to know about that person.
Female: You symbolize something in high school and you can't do much about that. . . . When I came here nobody knew me and I could start all over again.
Male: There are a lot of really good people here who, in high school, you didn't even give them a chance.
Female: You're willing to accept people who are a little bit different. People are more accepting all around.
Male: Yeah, if you talked to certain people in high school, you figure, "God, what will everyone think" or something.

Another predominant feature of this transitional period from hometown to campus is that students learn rather quickly that they have lost the bonds and common experiences that once held old friendships together:

Female: When you graduate, everybody leaves for school in August and says, "Oh, I'll write to you; we'll be friends; next summer we can come home and live together again." I went home for a vacation over Christmas, and people don't even want to give up time to spend with you because they have their own lives now. But up here—I really look forward to coming back because the people I live with here are the ones I'm closest to, and they understand everything. At home, they have no conception of what it is to go to college, what it is to study or anything. They just sit around and work and go out every night.

Female: It's funny like that, two of us out of my whole graduating class went to school out of the state. The other one is a guy I knew all through high school, and he knew of me but we didn't get to really know each other until our senior year. He started going out with one of my best friends, and now he is the one that keeps in touch with me and I keep in touch with him. I've found that out with a lot of my friends where I'd write, I'd call, and I'd get no response.... The two of us found out that going away to school was a big difference, and that's what made us a little bit more unique than everybody else.

Female: Something like that happened to me the first time I went home. I was all psyched and everything and I thought, "Great, I can see all my old friends and everything." It was just a weekend, and there was one other guy from my high school that goes here, and the funny thing is we never hung around together in high school, and I hardly see him at all here—once every three weeks or so. We ended up going out at home together. We don't even go out up here or anything. It's just that we found that nobody was responding, you know.

Male: Well, this environment breeds a different kind of friendship. It's a deeper relationship because we're living with our friends all the time.

Others expressed similar concerns and described a period in which they were "living two different lives" or functioning in "two different worlds." As their "celebrity status" diminishes, however, the brief visits home become increasingly less rewarding and less frequent. At the same time, new experiences and common interests with college friends expand, become more intimate, and eventually replace high school relationships. By their junior year, most students come to the realization that the campus community represents their "real home."

Commuting and community college students who have not left their family environment do not, of course, experience such a dramatic or sharply defined transitional period. For them, campus relationships are often casual and somewhat superficial. Closer friendships are limited to a couple of individuals met in classes or in visits to the coffee lounge and student union. Many older students would like more interaction but feel "foolish" or "out of place" when they initiate relationships with classmates who are half their age. The press for time is also a factor: "I go to work, come to school, and go back to work—continuous cycles. I don't have time to become friends with anybody or get that close."

Friendship patterns for traditional students on a residential campus are invariably a product of the campus living arrangement.

Male: It seems to me that probably the thing that determines your friendships is where you live. First of all, when you are a freshman you come to the residence hall. These are the people who are closest to you and will probably have a better chance of developing into your friends. After that, once you get to know the college and the places around, you can join a fraternity or get into a group with people in your own curriculum. But when you first start out, I'd say it would probably be the place where you live.

Female: I'd like to say something about living in the dorm. It's a really beautiful experience. You get to meet so many people that are so much different from you. Every person you meet, just about, is different. I learn things from being around other people and by talking to other people. Like someone from New York or Florida or somewhere else, they'll tell you about things there. I just learned a lot that I didn't know . . . I like to be around people because I always learn something, somehow.

Male: Yeah, you can meet different people. I was just used to one setting for eighteen years and, here, there are so many different cultures you can get to know. You have to learn how to deal with them, too.

Female: This type of situation is really neat because one of the most enjoyable things for me is to sit down and just talk with one person, individually. About anything. Just about different thoughts that we have and being exposed to different values and ideas. It gives me another way of looking at things but it also gives me a chance to either reaffirm that which I already believed right for me or say, "Hey, wait a minute; maybe something's wrong here. Maybe I really do need to take another look." It's a good experience to learn how to deal with people in general. When you're living in a dorm you're in with about forty other people. You get to know their habits and moods and you also learn how to deal with them. You learn how to get along with people. I think it's great to come from a home situation where you've been isolated, pretty much, and come here to a completely different situation where you have to learn.

Male: I don't live on campus, I stay at home. In a way, I think people that stay on campus have an advantage over me because of the fact that they're dealing with the people on their floor every day and, as far as meeting people, I'm sort of limited. Like when you're in a dormitory you know just about everybody on your floor, but for me, it's the people I meet in class and the people I meet on campus.

During the college years, friendships are strengthened and refined through such common interests as intramural sports, specialized groups, and extracurricular activities. Classroom contacts, however, are described by students a superficial acquaintances that seldom develop into responsive relationships. As one student remarked, "You couldn't describe them as friends or someone you could share your feelings with . . . you know a lot of people from classes but you really don't know them. You know their faces but that's about it." Most typically, then, freshman and sophomore students rarely have mutual academic experiences with members of their friendship group and, not surprisingly, the hot topics for discussions and bull sessions seldom involve intellectual concepts. Juniors and seniors have more interaction with individuals who are in the same curriculum, and some friendship patterns within major fields of study are evident. In addition to mutual academic and career interests, this phenomenon is a function of smaller class sizes and the simple fact that upperclass students may have a number of courses in common for a sequence of three or four consecutive semesters.

In general, however, students seem to genuinely regret the typical lack of communication with classmates. A few instructors will take time during the class sessions to conduct some get-acquainted exercises or simply have pairs of students get to know and introduce one another to the class. Such efforts were always praised. Classroom discussions and assignments or projects that encourage or even require students to interact were frequently mentioned as examples that made learning more human and more meaningful. Conversely, there was obvious resentment toward the routine of marching in and out of classes in robot-like fashion without opportunities to exchange ideas and feelings related to the course.

Relationships with Parents

Just as there are problems that students feel only peers can completely understand, there are needs that only parental love and admiration can fullfill. The familiarity, warmth, and memories that are embodied within the family itself contribute to a sense of comfort and security. As one woman puts it, "Whenever I go home, I appreciate it even more. I've started a ritual ever since I went to summer camp and had to sleep on a cot for two months. I come home and run upstairs and dive on my bed. I do that when I come home from school, too, because the beds in the dorms are really the pits! It's my ritual—as soon as I put my suitcase down—and my parents expect it. The food always tastes better, and the house always seems bigger. My mother always sits next to me for the first hour and touches me. It's kind of neat. I've really grown to understand my parents—like who they are as people. And I understand myself a lot more through knowing what kind of people they are. There is a lot of them in me, of course."

An occasional weekend at home, parental visits to campus, and even letters and telephone conversations seem to provide a continuing sense of identity and a reaffirmation of affection. After reflecting on their family relationships, many students concluded that the quality of communication and level of understanding is better now than it ever was in earlier years. "We're all closer now," "my mom has become my best friend," and "I can talk to my dad and he understands" were comments about relationships with parents. If there is a serious "generation gap" at the turn of this decade, it certainly is not perceived and articulated by students. These positive attitudes are due, in part, to the changing intensity of the relationships. Time together is usually for brief, pleasant visits, and the relationships do not have to endure all of the strains involved in day-to-day decisions and conflicts related to living under the same roof. The most significant variables, however, are the general feelings of trust and self-reliance that accompany a greater degree of personal independence.

Male: I feel better about being totally on my own. I don't have feelings like, "Oh, oh, it's all up to me." I kind of like to have to worry about what I'm going to buy, or if I'm going to be able to pay for my food. It just gives me a safer feeling, more secure. When I was younger, I had to depend on somebody because I wasn't old enough to do anything. So I kind of had bad feelings like, "What if this person were suddenly gone? What am I going to do?" There's always going to be someone gone, but as long as I'm still here I can take care of myself and that gives me a feeling of security.

Female: I agree that it feels kind of good to be independent. I've been pretty dependent all of my life—all the way through high school until I came down here. But now I have a work study job and everything is fine. . . . It feels so good because I'm taking a load off my parents, and it's like I'm doing something on my own. It makes me feel good because I did it for myself.

Male: Yeah, I know. My parents are a lot of trouble because they're too nice. They feel, for some reason, that they have to pay for my college. I've been working over the summer and during breaks, and I can help out a lot, but they don't want me to use my own money. They say, "You keep your money—save it. Like last night, I was talking to my mom on the phone and she says, "Do you want me to send you some more money?" And I go, "No, now just cool it." She says, "You know we're willing to pay for this." And I go, "Mom, will you just keep your money," because I feel like I'm too dependent on them. I don't have to be but they want me to be for some reason. It's like I'm their little boy who is getting away, I think.

One woman, as though she were addressing a group of parents at a freshman orientation session, made the following observation: "I know so many students who have to explain everything they do to their parents. "Have you been doing this" or "You should know better than that." That type of thing, you know. Let them be themselves; let them feel that they have room to breathe while they're in college. The only way they're going to learn is to experience it. . . . I feel sorry for them because their parents just don't seem to respect them at all. They don't give them any feeling of self-worth. The most important thing parents can give their child is to make them feel like a good person. When parents are always questioning their son or daughter, it is real obvious that they lack trust in them, and I just feel so sorry for those kids."

The struggle for independence was often framed around a major issue in the maturation process. Fewer parental behavior expectations, greater autonomy in decision making, and a general respect for their opinions and beliefs were all important factors discussed by students. But the most concrete and visible indication that complete self-reliance has not been achieved for many students is the undeniable financial dependence on their parents. The following unrelated excerpts from two students further demonstrate how this issue causes continued anxiety:

Male: I feel like I can't mess up because I figure that they're putting out all this money for me, and it's like I'm obligated. . . . I don't feel good about it, and I just wish I could raise the money so I wouldn't feel this way.

Female: I guess it's just the way I was raised. I don't like to ask for money—I hate it with a passion. In fact, I usually get overdrawn before I will ask my dad to put money in the account to cover bad checks. Instead of calling ahead of time, I wait as long as I can because I hate it so much.

From the student's point of view, perhaps the greatest obstacle to more communication with parents is their inability to understand or comprehend college life. Parents are often guilty of equating college and learning with achieving satisfactory grades. They do not seem to be aware of the pressures that students encounter within the campus culture. "They ask about my studies, and if that's going okay, they think that everything is automatically fine." There seems to be little understanding or even recognition of such common dynamics as all-nighters, drug use, time pressures, the dating scene, or simply "goofing-off to all hours of the morning." Women are often disheartened by a discrepancy of values regarding dating, marriage, and children, which can translate into feeling a need to explain about not "having a ring" by their senior year. It should be clear, however, than in spite of some misunderstandings and differences of opinion, most students were positive about their ability to communicate with parents.

Faculty Relationships

The most telling characteristic of meaningful faculty-student relationships is their scarcity. A general feeling among students is that the campus community consists of two communication networks: a student culture and a bureaucratic structure composed of faculty and administrators. There is little expectation that members of the "system" or "establishment" will view personal relationships with students as a high priority, and in reality very few students can identify a faculty member with whom they have established a close relationship. The term "friend" is seldom, if ever, mentioned in the context of faculty encounters. Much of the difficulty is a stereotyped perception that students have of faculty members as intimidating, stuffy intellectuals:

Female: I haven't gotten close to one of my teachers. I haven't had that many large classes, but I don't know if I have the initiative to go up and really get to know them. The only profs that I've had have been TAs, and I admire a lot of profs you know, and I think they're really great teachers. They're interesting and I can respect them, but I just haven't been able to get close enough to really get to know them.

Male: It's hard to get to know them. I had a couple of profs last year who I really respected. They were really intelligent and had some great ideas, but they were so far over my head. I felt if I really tried to talk to them down on my level, you know—I felt really uncomfortable. I felt like I was just some jerk taking up this guy's time—this brilliant professor or something.

Faculty members are often viewed as unaccepting of student problems, unconcerned about their learning difficulties, and somewhat condescending. As one student explained: "I'm not about to go to them and prove that I'm a bigger dummy than they already think." Students frequently described the idea of approaching one of their instructors as scary, threatening, or demeaning. Some students "don't have the courage" to ask a question in class, let alone make an appointment for an individual conference. Others feel that the risk involved far outweighs the potential benefits.

Many students do, however, feel a need to "play the student role" according to their interpretation of the prescribed rules for academic gamesmanship. In simple terms, they view their task as figuring out what each professor wants and then delivering it. With a better grade in the course or a future letter of recommendation as motivation, students may project an image of their interest through visible attentiveness during lectures or active participation in class discussions. If they perceive that establishing some sort of relationship with the professor might help, they will attempt to do that. As one student explains the game: "Grades are the reason that relationships with teachers are important. You can go either way. You may want to get to know him to get a better grade or, if he's a terrible bore, you may want to stay away so that he doesn't know who you are when he looks at your papers. You've got to figure out which is to your advantage." Similarly a woman comments: "When it comes time to look for a job and you need that recommendation, where do you go? If you don't get to know any faculty or anybody while you're in college, who do you ask for a recommendation?"

At the same time, the very mention of academic advisors would invariably be met with a roar of laughter:

Male: What about academic advisors?
Female: Is there such a thing on this campus?
Male: My advisor? They divide accounting professors up to advise students. Maybe I see mine once a semester and he didn't even show last semester. I go again and he's a half hour late. So this semester I go to his office, and he's too busy. He sloughs me off on a stranger. My advisor was a stranger, but this guy I'd never even seen before. Now he's taking care of all the accounting students. He allows ten minutes for each of us.
Female: In the Art Department, they decided to get smart and do all the advising from 9:00 to 4:00 on one day during registration week. No classes, so all the instructors would be down in this one room and you just run in there and they'll advise or help. So they type up a little sign that indicates all of the mandatory courses they threw in at the last minute. You read the sign, get a signature, and leave. That's what they call advising.

There are notable exceptions, but most students seem to agree that advisors do not have the time or interest to do a competent job and they emphatically deny any implication that such a system is designed to help students or establish a foundation for personal, meaningful relationships. Students also acknowledge, however, that a "bad advisor can ruin you," and they warn younger students to "check things out for themselves" or consult with upperclass students in the same major who know the ropes. This general distrust of the advising process is constantly reinforced by both real and imagined tales of failure:

Male: This is my fifth year here. My advisor . . . had me taking Checkers 101! Now they say I've got to come back next semester because of this math requirement that he didn't know about, and nobody ever told me. I feel sorry for the hundreds of students who will be going through that broadcasting sequence, and he's the only advisor. And that's pitiful.
Female: My advisor is twenty-four, and he just graduated from another school. He doesn't really know anything about the system here. I've been here for four years, and I suppose that I should be able to fill out my own forms. But my biggest fear is that on May 14 somebody is going to tap on my shoulder while I'm in line to graduate: "Excuse me, you're three credits short." It's just this horrible fear. My parents are up there in this huge

coliseum looking for me through binoculars, and I'm back in some room crying my eyes out.

On a positive note, the college environment is actually more personable and responsive than students had anticipated. Three freshman students, for example, discount some of the things that they had been told by high school teachers, and indicate that student initiative can help to establish faculty contacts:

Female: Before I came, I heard so many horror stories about college professors. One teacher had a story every day about the horrors of college. Nobody gives a damn about you, and you just might as well hang things up if you can't think on your own. If you're having problems, most of the time, they don't care. But I haven't found that here at all. I don't know that many of my teachers because I haven't had too much of a problem so far in my classes. But the classes where I did have problems, there was someone willing to help me out. I didn't expect that at all. I had been pumped so full of horror stories that I thought, "God what am I getting myself into." On the other hand, I have this math lab that's so impersonal that I just hate to go to that class. Everyone is in a little box in the room and you have 100 people in there. I hate going to that class—it's an effort for me. I just hate to have to sit there for an hour. All I see is this book in front of me and three white walls. You just don't have contact with anyone. It just makes for a very boring period.

Male: When she was talking about the horrors, I was thinking about my high school. They told me that I'd only be a number. That's the only thing you'd be is a number. Nobody would know your first name, your last name, you're just a social security number. Somebody else could come into class and take your test and they wouldn't know any difference if they used your social security number. I find that not to be true. In the majority of my classes they know my name. In my biology class—like everything has two sides to it—we've got 150 people in there, and all he knew was my number. It depends on the class and how large it is.

Male: I was told the same thing when I was in high school. They said that you'll only be a number in college. But when I came the people here said that "It's up to you" and that's true. Most of my teachers, I have to go to them. The more I go to them and the more I talk to them, it seems like the better it is when I get to class. Because when I go to class, I sit down and just listen to the teachers and I say, "Aw, this teacher's boring." I go see him after class and talk to him, he's a different person. . . . If you go to the teacher and talk to him, that releases some of the tension. I feel that when I take time to get to know the professor, that I'm one step ahead of the other people. Most students just come to class and they leave. As far as relationships with faculty members go, right now it's okay. I'm not having any problems.

Thus, while many students complain that professors should make an effort to know them, others who reach out to the faculty report satisfying results. These contacts, however, are usually linked to a specific academic or administrative problem situation. Psychological counselors and residence hall advisors are often viewed as helpful, as well as classroom instructors and academic deans. Teaching methods that encourage discussion and personal opinions are often cited as positive factors in making the instructors more approachable. Similarly, faculty members who are informal or self-disclosing are perceived as more likable and human. The classroom image is a key variable to out-of-class contacts:

> I can get along a lot better with professors that keep me relaxed. Those guys in the economics department know their stuff—if they could just be comfortable with people. I think there's a lot of difference when you have a guy up there talking to you who is relaxed, opposed to the guy coming on in a three-piece Botany 500 suit, with his custom attaché case, engraved Cross pen set, and the whole bit. He puts in his fifty minutes and leaves. I say, "Man I wouldn't go talk to you for anything, mister." They're talking at you instead of to you. . . . Last semester I had to go up and get my final grade in economics before I went home. I was looking at the grades posted on the professor's door when he walked up. He grabbed me and we sat down and talked for an hour. I just kicked myself for not doing it earlier. There's a guy who knows his stuff, and it was the most enjoyable class because it was new material, and he was really well prepared. I'm just sorry that I didn't go in and talk to him earlier because he was a whole different person out of the classroom situation.

While satisfying faculty-student relationships are an infrequent part of contemporary college life, there are signs that students are receptive, that educators want to be helpful, and that present attitudinal barriers could be overcome.

Summary

For most students, the transition from hometown to collegiate friendship groups is a smooth and satisfying experience. Peer relationships on campus, particularly those developed within living units, provide powerful, important support groups within the student culture. At the same time, students characterize parental relationships in predominantly positive, understanding, and affectionate terms even though they feel and recognize the strains of becoming more independent and autonomous human beings. Out-of-classroom relationships with faculty members are rare, and students seldom describe them as either helpful or friendly. The traditional system of academic advisement is universally rejected as a mechanism to foster meaningful relationships, and, in fact, was often cited as evidence that faculty members are either too busy, uninterested, or simply unwilling to spend time with students.

Students claim to appreciate the educational advantages of living in a pluralistic campus environment, yet minority populations are more tolerated than embraced, more feared than understood.

Multicultural Relationships and Pluralistic Life-Styles

David A. DeCoster
Phyllis Mable

Students frequently report that college has broadened their view of life by exposing them to a much more diverse community than they had previously experienced. This belief seems to be sincere and is often articulated convincingly, as in the following discussion:

Female: If you had the choice over, would you choose a college like this one that has all these different people or would you choose a college with a student body that is more similar to yourself?
Female: I like it the way it is here.
Male: I have thoroughly enjoyed knowing some of the young white students and young black students. It's just a fantastic experience for me to be able to know such a diversity of people.
Female: If you're limited in experiences, you can become prejudiced. You're not going to understand other people's feelings as well.
Male: Different people tell you about their lives and you tell them about your life—and we're all learning something. I've learned to appreciate and admire some of the older students with families who are struggling to work and go to school at the same time.

D. A. DeCoster and P. Mable (Eds.), *New Directions for Student Services: Understanding Today's Students,* no. 16. San Francisco: Jossey Bass, 1981.

Similarly, a white female and a Hispanic male describe cordial, healthy interactions that have evolved with black students through mutual academic interests:

Female: There are a lot of black students in the mental health curriculum, and I've gotten close to some of them, whereas I never had the opportunity before. We have had problems with mixing in some classes but I think that we've handled it fairly well. We sit down and talk to each other in the lounge, and there are several students that I'm really glad that I have had the experience of knowing.
Male: I also have quite a few blacks in my classes who I socialize with as far as school goes. We stand in the hallway and talk or have a coffee together. We get along fine. Of course, I was born and raised with blacks, and I'm in one of the minority groups too. My point is that the school should not give the impression that the level in any class is lower because of minorities or lower because of women or because of a higher age group. That sort of thing doesn't help anyone.

While students repeatedly promote the educational and social advantages of a heterogeneous campus community, only a small percentage actually come to know people who are very different from themselves. Some students, in fact, proclaimed with apparent pride that most people would accept a Tri Delt or an Alpha Chi who dated an independent. Opportunities for meaningful interaction and communication among students of different cultural and ethnic backgrounds is certainly not a routine part of college life:

Female (white): I think that it's hard for people to start talking about racial concerns. When we first started this discussion, I realized that I hadn't talked about these things much or even thought about them. Most of us don't have that many black friends, and we don't have a chance to really talk with other people. I was hesitant to even get into the conversation today. I can only imagine what the communications are like on a national scale.
Male (white): A discussion like this rarely happens and, when they do, everybody usually ends up walking away with different impressions.
Female (black): I don't want to hear it.
Male (white): At least they're being exposed to each others feelings and this is necessary. If anything is going to happen, we have to understand what each other is thinking.
Female (black): Well, we have to talk. Like when you said earlier that you weren't sure what blacks meant when they call someone a Tom. I had two white roommates last year, and they were really anxious and curious about what I was like and about the black culture. "What's that for? What's

this for?" And I would ask them the same things. That's the only way we have to learn. If you want to know something, you have to ask.

This lack of communication is fostered by factors other than opportunity and convenience. Examples of true empathy, understanding, and personal compassion are all but lost within a prevailing attitude of indifference toward minority students by the white majority. Thus, the predominant mood can be characterized as one of tolerance and neglect which, at times, is accentuated by acts of clear and overt racism. Students on almost every campus identified a recent major conflict between white and minority students: cross burnings, territorial disputes over lounge or dining hall space, name calling and fights when all-minority and all-white teams compete in intramural sports, landlord discrimination, and bitter arguments over the type of music to be played at campus dances. Such incidents create publicity, tension, and controversy but seem to be simply "weathered" rather than resolved. Likewise, attempts by minority students to effect changes are not met with much enthusiasm. Although not always articulated so harshly, the reactions of two white students to a proposal for a Black Student Union captures a typical feeling:

Male: There aren't very many black students other than people coming in on athletic scholarships or Africans that are on some type of exchange program. They don't amount to a significant portion of the student body, and why should they have any special privileges. There is nothing about our present facilities that exclude the blacks any more than the whites. A student union building is a student union building, and they can use it just as well as we can. We can't start giving special privileges to ethnic groups just because they're ethnic groups. . . . I don't see why more money should be diverted for their use. If we're going to give them a free ride and a meal ticket, then why should we give them anything more?

Male: I resent their making demands. When they're offered those scholarships, they're given a full understanding of what the college has to offer in terms of student union groups, clubs, curriculum, and all that. They know what they're getting, so why do they accept something only to come here and attempt to change it? It's just an outright display of trying to stir up trouble.

A student at another institution provides additional insight that accurately captures the state of affairs at many schools:

Male (white): My impression of this campus is that we do not have a good sensitivity to the needs of cultural minorities. What we do with minorities is we tolerate them and, as long as they don't raise any hell or raise any issues, they're okay. "They're good people." But, by God, the moment that this campus would elect five Native American senators or five Chicano or black senators, and they would start wielding a little power, you would see some different reactions.

And finally, three women who recognize the importance of honest communication share some experiences that foster misunderstandings at a midwestern institution:

Female (white): I just wish there could be more individual communication. It seems like there are so many groups on this campus. There are the black people, the white people, the high smokers, the foreigners—and everyone sets up these barriers. It's so hard to break through to them. It's so frustrating because when we get together we're really inhibited by a big group, and there's no discussion. And then the first thing you know, you're in the middle of a confrontation.
Female (white): Sometimes people try to communicate, and it doesn't work out. They say, "The heck with it, I'm not going to try again."
Female (black): That's right. I was in the cafeteria, and this one white dude came by with a friend and says so I can hear it, "Hey, you going to the Ku Klux Klan meeting tonight." That just turned me off, and I was so mad and so upset that people could be that way. Then the next white person I see gets the results—feels my anger.

The latter incident exemplifies the type of personal indignities that minority students must sustain on a continuing basis. While the majority of white students seem to find some security with an attitude of ambivalence and indifference, many minority students are constantly confronted with expressions of racist anger and hatred that challenge their coping skills and patience. The following unrelated statements are indicative:

Female (black): I had this girl friend, and we used to do things together, and she was so cute. These two guys walked up to her one day and called her a nigger lover. Whenever we went somewhere at night, people would sit and stare at us. It made me mad because when people stare at me, they're saying I'm less of a person than they are, and I'm apt to turn around and say something to them. Like we were in a restaurant one night, and this lady sat there and stared at us as if we were dirt. I just turned around and looked at her and said, "May I help you? Is there something you want at this table?" She dropped her head and looked the other way. Stuff like that really makes me mad. People are people no matter what color their skin is.
Male (white): I know this guy in our dorm who is an Indian. He's really a nice kid and everyone relates to him really well, but off-campus he's really having a tough time. It's starting to bother him, and he's finding it

hard to deal with the tension. Therefore, he feels restricted to campus because people treat him so harshly in town. It's affecting his social life and he's depressed a lot of times. People in this town have the attitude that the only good Indian is a dead one.

Male (black): Well, I have a lot of white friends, and I get along with people in general. When I first came here, it was pretty cool. Then I started noticing things. When I walk on campus, people look at me like I'm from a different world, and if I speak, they start digging for pennies and turn their heads. After awhile you just go your own way and they go their way.

Female (white): I just hate walking down the street and passing these small, smelly, greasy foreigners. And they come on to you—"get in the car with me"—and I just hate that. And it's just not one group, it's all of the Arabs. . . . I can't stand those Africans always asking you to dance—they can't even talk English.

Stereotypes and fear of people who are different often form the basis for attitudes and behavior for other minority life-styles on campus. Gay students, for example, are usually labeled with such terms as queers, fags, funny people, or switch hitters, and most students simply prefer not to discuss their feelings in detail. The following discussion embodies some of the naive stereotypes that are prevalent:

Female: I was totally shocked when I found out. I never thought anyone here would be homosexual . . . I came across it from playing women's sports. The way I feel about it is that I don't care if they're homosexual, just so they don't have any actions in front of me. They can go and be homosexual on their own but, if they are homosexual in front of me, I get sick—I just do. But I guess I can't condemn them for it.

Male: I feel the same way because people are going to be different in general. I was told that a person who is queer is one of the best friends you can have if he doesn't bother you.

Male: I come from a big city, and I run into a lot of them. You can't go condemning everyone you meet because at a big university it's an everyday thing, and they are sticking up for their rights. We can't condemn them here either as long as they don't attack.

In general, students feel threatened by homosexuals of their own sex, they do not lend support to the gay liberation movement, and they do not expect to be "hassled about it." The typical response is, "They can do what they want but they should stay to themselves—stay in the closet." Some students confide that exposure to gay life-styles caused them to question or rethink their own sexual identity. Many feel more secure and comfortable with their gay counterparts since being exposed to them on campus. Attitudes toward other minority groups of students are somewhat the same. It is generally felt, for example, that adult learners and commuting students do not need special facilities or attention. Financial pressures were frequently cited as the reason for not considering additional programs or facilities. Most agreed that ramps should be built for disabled students and that blind people require special considerations, however, few expressed real insight or empathy for the handicapped. There is also some agreement that all students should have the right to an education but, again, educationally disadvantaged students or "one percentile types" are often discussed in a sarcastic or joking way. Finally, men seem irritable about women's rights and complain about affirmative action policies that create reverse discrimination. The following argument began when a woman suggested the need for a Women's Center on campus:

Male: What do you think a women's center would entail?

Female: It would be a place where I could go to sit around or rap or just do what I want with other women. I would feel comfortable going there.

Male: That would be discriminatory.... It's sort of ridiculous to have a male center, a female center, a black female center, you know, whatever.

Female: No, no, no. Well, white male Americans are certainly not discriminated against. They are masters.

Male: In my major, they are.

Female: What's your major?

Male: Occupational therapy.

Female: Well, they're the last ones in the world to be discriminated against.

Male: You think so?

Female: Yes, that's bull.

Male: If I tried to get a job right now, I'd be one of the last ones considered for hiring because they have to have a quota of blacks and a quota of women. If there's still room for me, I might get hired.

Female: Yeah, but what they're saying and what really happens—there is a big difference. Since equal pay has come up, women's pay has actually dropped in relation to men's salaries.... I'm not saying that people should fill quotas, but women shouldn't be discriminated against because they are women. And just because they're women, they shouldn't be hired for less money.

Male: So now you want separate but equal facilities. It's no longer integration, it's just like segregation.

Female: I would just like a place to go to be with other women. If men were allowed, what's to keep them from taking over like they usually do?

Male: I think that's paranoid.

Female: If you and I applied for the same job, you would probably get hired or I would get hired for a lower pay.

Male: You would get hired.

Female: Maybe because they could afford to hire me and couldn't afford you.
Male: Maybe they would need a secretary.

Students who are affiliated with the growing interest in Bible study and prayer groups on campus were also identified as a significant minority group. Like others, these individuals are generally accepted, and most students feel comfortable with the rights of others to religious expression. The problem comes, however, when religious activities involve preaching, converting others, or proselytizing. At that point, they are likely to be called "born again Jesus freaks who should keep their beliefs to themselves." Nonetheless, the Campus Crusade and other religious groups are active at most institutions, and members often form factions within residence halls and greek houses that can hardly be ignored.

All things considered, college students verbalize an accepting attitude toward cultural minority students as well as other students who exemplify backgrounds and life-styles different from their own. On closer examination, although they seem to appreciate living in a pluralistic campus community, they prefer involvement and interaction on their terms. Minority individuals are left with almost the total burden for accommodation and adjustment to the majority culture. As one white male flatly stated, "This institution was created by a predominately WASP society to meet their needs. That's just the way it is." Majority students are not very supportive of new programs or changes in the environment that are proposed by minority groups and typically are not sensitive to prejudicial or racist behavior directed at others. Thus, there seems to be a campus atmosphere of uneasy survival for students who present different orientations, needs, and life-styles—especially for ethnic minorities. Furthermore, their precarious position has aggravated dehumanizing personal experiences and periodic confrontations with the dominant white community. Multicultural communications are minimal and misunderstandings frequent. The possibility that intense feelings of alienation will ignite more active future confrontations is certainly present.

A few additional observations may be noteworthy. For one reason or another, to most students the term "minority" means "black." Therefore, Hispanic, Native American, and other ethnic minority groups on campus receive relatively little attention. A number of factors may contribute to this perception: the black population is typically larger, the history of black involvement in state and national political roles is usually more publicized, and black students may simply be more visible on campus and more vocal in expressing their concerns.

Another obvious dynamic is that students did not participate in the discussions of this topic with the same enthusiasm and openness demonstrated by the other groups. Comments were often superficial, observations were guarded, and white students seemed inhibited, intimidated, or fearful—

especially when ethnic minority students were participating in the discussion. This all suggests that the topics involving multicultural relationships were difficult for students to address, which may well be a function of the frustrations that were verbalized regarding a lack of cross-cultural communication and understanding. Finally, various minority groups did not have the opportunity to explore these topics solely from their perspective, nor did ethnic minority students have the chance to discuss relationships with other minority groups as a separate cross-cultural issue.

Summary

The concepts of increasing growth and development through meaningful contacts within a pluralistic campus community is a complex issue. Students verbalize the experience of learning through contact with people of cultures, backgrounds, and life-styles that are different from their own. Further analysis, however, reveals that cross-cultural communication is minimal and superficial and that misunderstandings and feelings of suspicion permeate such relationships. Examples of sexism, ethnocentrism, stereotyped images, and overt racism continue to plague college communities and to threaten the dream of a unified multicultural environment.

Most college students pursue personal development as part of the collegiate experience but choose to ignore those social and political issues they perceive as having little bearing on their personal success.

Social and Political Issues

Phyllis Mable
David A. DeCoster

Students want to be well informed, reinforced in their personal convictions, successful in careers, and knowledgeable as citizens in a participatory society. On that assumption, colleges are creating opportunities for learning by experience as well as for appreciating societal requirements. Students want to grow intellectually, build self-confidence, increase capabilities, and achieve personal recognition and fulfillment, but they have little time, concern, and interest for social and political issues that torment the modern world. Students want to be "rich" and they want to be "somebody." Social and political issues command little attention as students arrange their collegiate lives according to ambitious, single-minded, and durable personal aspirations.

Central to the current view of social and political issues on college campuses is an opportunity for students to develop skills and techniques that enhance human relations and help them cope with the uncertainties of life. The larger question is whether students who are firmly committed to their own self-indulgence can in some fashion maximize their personal development, especially when the job market is unpredictable, the bureaucracy concentrates authority with a few selected officials, and the media determine political priorities. Students are somewhat preoccupied with trying to find the right mix of grades, careers, and successes. They search for strength, humor, and hope, and they wonder about society. Their ultimate concern is personal development that will enable them to cope with life after college.

D. A. DeCoster and P. Mable (Eds.), *New Directions for Student Services: Understanding Today's Students,* no. 16. San Francisco: Jossey Bass, 1981.

Personal Development

From a student perspective, personal development is self-understanding, self-reliance, and interpersonal communication with peers and role models. In fact, there was a fair amount of agreement among students: in high school, teachers and parents made decisions and influenced directions; in college, students are responsible for choices in an atmosphere perceived to be more open and honest with significantly higher stakes. No matter how many times students questioned the future, personal development was too important ever to qualify as mediocre. Personal development includes such issues as "who I am," "what I stand for," and "what I value," rather than the expressions of a governing establishment or needs relating to a set of social and political concerns that barely existed on college campuses in the late seventies and early eighties.

Since the massive changes of the sixties, students have been side-stepping social and political reforms in favor of relatively serene and quiet living. But they are not impassive. They are collecting themselves while looking for a future and a purpose. Many students report with conviction that the freshman year is the big, determining year: "College, especially the freshman year, is a good time to learn. There isn't pressure from the outside world, there is a lot of freedom, and there isn't punishment for experimenting with relationships and behaviors." An older student reports that college is necessary emotionally and financially for advancement. She says, "Development is greatly needed. What high schools and colleges teach today is different, new, and technical, but I want to develop myself inwardly and become more independent." Thus, students link their personal and academic lives with an abundance of what everyone wants and what so many others have, and take for granted.

Students discuss personal development in ways that illustrate the issues:

Male: Some people feel they're here just to study, and some people are here just for the social life. I was in pharmacy originally, and I know I studied more than I do now. My priorities have changed. It is important to meet people and get involved. I know people who study all the time, and they seem happy. I know people who don't study all the time, and they are happy too. That's what is so great about being here. You can choose which way you want to go.

Female: Well, if the object of being in school is to get a really good job, then I feel that you're going to have to go through some sort of suffering. You cannot have a social life and really put all of your effort into studying. Studying really hard and getting good grades gets the job you want. You must pay your dues.

Male: I disagree with the suffering thing. I haven't studied myself into oblivion since I've been here. My grades are good, but I put as much emphasis on attempting to work with my career and with the people who have taught me and given me an opportunity outside the classroom. You're not learning just from your courses, and I don't think grades are going to earn you the job.

Female: I was always under the impression that at least half of what you get in class just takes up time. The bulk of the material you learn is general knowledge that you're not going to use in your job. Going to school is only half of what you're here for. Learning to interact with others, living away from home, meeting people, and finding friends are the most important parts of education. Meeting people and making friends determines the type of person you will be. If you come to school with the sole attitude that you're going to do good work in classes and get a job, then I think you're missing half of college.

Male: After high school, I thought I knew where my head was at: what I wanted, what I planned to do for my major and career, what I valued. It finally hit me during my freshman year. I didn't know what I thought about many things. I didn't know how I felt about certain people. It was hard to go through something like that. A lot of people go through changes before they graduate, not just academic changes, but personal.

Students talked among themselves about a kind of operational optimism, a sense that doing your best required laying yourself open, making yourself enthused about dealing with school, people, and life. Both new students and older students seek to find the best in themselves.

Another group of students describes the issues:

Female: Personal development is an ongoing experience that lasts throughout life. College opens the doors. I see areas where I am lacking . . . areas where I have strengths. The academic experience is necessary because it exercises my mind, but the most important part of college is talking with people . . . going to parties, Bible study, and bars. Living around students gives me a totally new outlook on life.

Female: To understand yourself, you must understand people and figure out who you want to be around, what you want to do. Here at college, there is a wide range of people with whom to associate. All of this brings out the real you.

Male: College helps me to decide for myself what is right, what is wrong. I am surrounded with people—all different kinds. They make you change. I am free to question stuff at school. I know what I've been taught, but I have to change personally as well.

A couple of changes from the trends of the sixties are obvious: the time of rebelling against money and power and the movement to more natural life-styles is over. Students aspire to personal happiness that embodies the material comforts of the present decade. They exercise ambitious drive; they want more money, opportunity, power, and freedom. They want new sensitivity and awareness, effective communication and interpersonal relationships, and a sense of identity that is constantly reassessed.

Social Issues

In the past few years, some elusive elements of social concern have faded as students focus on their own survival and opportunities. College students of the sixties and seventies, who refused to accept the common verdict that certain achievements and ideals were impossible to attain, appealed for civil rights, an end to the Vietnam War, equal rights for women, changes in abortion and marijuana laws, ecological preservation, and conservation of energy. In a number of memorable instances, their social consciousness stirred the entire nation. At present, however, there is only a trace of the restless idealism that once captured the imagination of the younger generation and forced the nation and world to listen.

Some students today say that they condemn racism and sexism, oppose draft registration, support gay rights, despise crime, and disapprove of the new, conservative drinking laws. While students hold out some hope for a more relevant and compassionate society, they also describe themselves as uncommitted, ineffective, and powerless.

Male: Students are more concerned about their education than the shape of the world. They really don't care about what goes on nationally. Are students apathetic? Not really. They are just concerned about what they can do for themselves. They feel that they have to grow and help themselves before they can help others. Anyhow, they can't do much about the problems . . . poverty, racism, crime, women's rights, energy.

Male: Students don't have the money and political pressure to do anything about problems. They are wrapped up with their own lives . . . finances, inflation. . . . When I get my own life straight, then I will worry about other people and their problems.

Female: I want to work, make money, and live nice. Hopefully, I can do volunteer work at some point. I have to get me straight first . . . then I can do for the world.

Female: A lot of what we want to do has to wait until we are out in the real world. Do we really understand the world? I have to prove myself before people will accept my ideas. I've only been to school. How can I know?

Another group of students explains similar attitudes but in different ways:

Male: At college, I am involved in my own life. We are geographically away from cities, and we have almost no interaction with outside people. We live on an island, and social and political issues don't affect us directly. There is hardly time to read newspapers and listen to the news.

Male: Yeah, I agree. It seems like this campus is a little city set off by itself with its own police, its own fire department, and its own government . . . run completely for the purpose of getting people degrees. It seems like a little city that runs itself . . . when you're here, you don't really have to concern yourself with anything going on outside. We can watch the news and see what's going on, but you know it doesn't involve you on a day-by-day basis.

Female: When I came to campus, I was a freshman, I was in space shock. . . . I was really alienated from the outside. But I don't feel that way any more. There are things on this campus that fulfill me enough. This is my world. It doesn't bother me that much, not knowing what's going on outside.

Often content to endorse the status quo, students have accepted the position that social issues are not necessarily resolved—and their attitudes seldom reflect passion or even authentic interest. Says one student, representative of her peers, "If it doesn't threaten me, it doesn't bother me." Some students ponder their responsibility and become overwhelmed with political and economic structures associated with governmental controls. It is not surprising that students, as well as nonstudents, try to assign responsibility to someone they perceive as possessing authority. Well-being is a natural outgrowth of the student character—ebullient, romantic, ready to defend individualism, and ironic enough to look forward to governmental regulation. Students discuss this combination of feelings and emotions:

Female: Restrictions—constant legislation of morality by the government—gripe me. I don't like the government telling me what I can do about abortion, drinking, or smoking pot. Who says "Big Daddy" knows what's right for the masses?

Male: Busing is another problem. When it's reasonable, it's good—more like the real world. The world will never be all blacks or all whites. We will never be totally integrated as long as one group dominates the other. If it weren't for the Civil Rights Act, nothing would be different.

Female: The government regulates busing. Why doesn't the government regulate parents! Parents won't live with each other—why force busing on the children. Kids are thrown together, and then they go back to separate communities . . . that's where the problem is. That's what is neat about college . . . classes and activities are together . . . we take showers together! That's what it's all about.

Male: I hate the idea of institutions legislating moral judgments. I want to create something . . . I want to do something for all black people.

I want to be best in what I want to be. I want to give blacks something to emulate. Everything else is incidental.

Female: That's unfair. Blacks are upset because they think whites don't care. Aren't you doing the same thing?

Male: There is a big imbalance now. I want to put black people in jobs. . . . I want the blacks to succeed. I want to be there to let them in on the action.

A combination of beliefs, coalescing at an opportune moment, leads to philosophical considerations, among them: humanism, individualism, and altruism. As one student explains, "If you want to be a number, okay. Or you can fight just as easily. You can be an individual. Do what you think is right. Don't blame things on others. You can make yourself and others happy." These students conclude this discussion on social issues:

Male: True, you can do what you want.

Female: Doesn't everyone do what he or she wants. We are all our own individuals within very broad limits.

Female: Who fights society? We do it to ourselves. We conform to a world that we have made . . . we are responsible.

Male: What are the things you worry about?

Female: I worry about the health of myself and my family. I worry about my family and the people closest to me.

Intentionally articulate about their beliefs, students have different priorities now, and they have "too many things tugging at them to get involved." At the present time, the predominant student desire is to excel, excel, excel.

Political Issues

Again and again, students maintain that there are no real political issues. Says one student, "Everyone is more middle-of-the-road now." More telling portents are those subtle worries, apprehensions, and fears that students encounter as they prepare for the job search. Essentially, students know about high interest rates, troublesome inflation, and persistent unemployment—American dilemmas that seem to render them helpless. Reactions to political issues range from "students are interested in personal activities" to "politics is not what is going on here" and finally to "this campus is very laid back." One student summarizes the mood: "Hardly anyone is involved in politics."

The following commentary among students highlights several distinctions:

Male: It's true we do occupy ourselves with what we are going to do for a job. Working and making money are important because we are used to certain middle-class standards of living. Yet a teacher who graduated in 1962 said that she was promised teaching jobs in her junior year. That's how bad they needed people. Anyone coming out of college could get a job. That changes your whole orientation and allows you to have time and freedom to think about other things. I could probably be attracted to some political issues but to become concerned about energy when you're used to having a color television and a car seems unimportant. Getting a job is what's important because I have to pay for the television and car. So I think that although we don't concern ourselves with social and political issues, other things are just as real to us. They represent obstacles and seem just as important.

Female: I think it's a more individualized, personalized concern. Unless there's something oppressing a large group of us, there is no reason to come together and explode. There is never enough of an issue.

Male: Why don't students get involved? They don't seem to be really involved in anything, whether it's a dance or a keg party. Even when it comes down to questioning where their money is going or how it is being spent . . . they don't seem to care. They hit one brick wall and they stop.

Female: I don't think there's really that many students who do that. I'm sure there are some. Personally, I'm not extremely active around here. I'm here for the education . . . a few activities are okay but only constructive ones. I don't get involved with anything that doesn't directly affect me.

Nobody is sure if many—or any—older students will actually seek to bring political issues back to the campus. One older student describes a glimmer of concern among his peers: "I hope to have an impact. People have to take control. When we have competent people in office, then others shape up. How can we make changes . . . through career choice. Education is the opportunity. Give me one generation of young, fertile minds. Plant the seed and watch it grow." Another older student believes that real education is between the old and young—on a one-to-one basis. She says, "Education will miss its golden opportunity if extracurricular and curricular experiences fail to utilize student resources—where the young learn from the old and the old learn from the young." This is an approach that has not been tried very much in education. The quality of American life for years to come may rest on taking some educational risks in the hope of getting results.

The Mood of Today's Students

Looming over every current discussion of college students is deep concern about the approaching five-figure tuition costs for some of the nation's schools. Rising costs send chills to the hearts and pocketbooks of hardpressed students and parents all over the country. Concurrently, college graduates are no longer members of an elite group. For these and other reasons, college students are forecasting tones and methods that will dominate the college scene: competition for grades, systematic career selection, realistic job prospects and opportunities. In conjunction with these very real economic flash points, students are strongly interested in developing themselves personally, deepening their capacity for relationships with other people, and determining a blend of meaningful leisure interests, career directions, and life-style choices.

The mood of college students is accurately described by an older student: "We're career-minded. Articles in magazines and newspapers talk constantly about unemployment, even for college graduates. Really, a lot of people are going to technical schools or degree schools because of the career concerns." A younger student explains the same mood: "Students are into careers. Some people go to college because their parents went to college or because their parents want them to go. However, most want to go to college because if you don't, you won't make it all the way." And, another student describes a similar feeling: "Jobs are college students' social issue. Like all of a sudden you are a senior. So, what am I going to do? Do I want to go to grad school?" Another group of students discuss the issues related to careers and jobs:

Male: College students today are more professional than they were in the sixties. Students aren't as passionate about issues. They are more concerned about getting jobs. They are also more conservative than they were before.

Male: A few students today worry about small issues. The issues are far less significant than they were years ago. Students are so career-oriented. They want to establish themselves in society. I think we're very materialistic.

Female: I think college students are more content than they were when everyone was fighting for civil rights and demonstrating for the end of the Vietnam War; the whole country is more content. People today are security-minded because the economy is so schizoid. There isn't as much security as we once thought there was. Students worry about jobs that they may or may not have when they get out of college.

Female: Today, the mood is finding out what't going on, investigating what's going on, and finding out what you're doing before you do it. I think it's reflected in college students. People want to look into things more. They're not just letting things ride by—they're simply not so easily swept up and away by every issue that comes along.

Despite the universal lack of interest in social and political issues, students remain concerned. Those who believe that the present college generation will determine what the world will look like at the turn of the century—and who realize the limits of control—wonder how their peers will proceed. As one student notes, "It's both neat and scary. No one wants to take responsibility." Another student talks about change, control, and power: "right now, I don't think I have any control as far as doing anything substantial. There are a lot of problems with world affairs, but everything is so vast and so involved. I think that a lot of things can be improved through education. We need to help people understand a little more of what's going on. Maybe, we should try to get rid of our own greed. The only way I know is by educating the people better."

Students respond with readiness of spirit and emotional restlessness. They want education that causes people to think and be open, lifelong learning, self-fulfillment, and equal access to life. Claims one student who sets himself apart from his peers: "College students do have the power. We're going to be tomorrow's business leaders, tomorrow's lawyers, tomorrow's workers. If we are educated and sensitive to some of the problems, then we will have the power, the responsibility, to solve them."

And, finally, students insist—indeed prove—that they have requirements in developing confidence and identity, interpersonal sensitivity and relationships, intelligence and physical competence. This discussion illustrates these constructs:

Female: How important to your development is knowing yourself? How do you go about knowing yourself?

Male: If anyone had the answer to knowing yourself, they would have the key to unlocking a lot of problems. Like I said before, you can't really learn to like or love other people unless you like or love yourself.

Male: If I look back on these last four college years, I'd have to say that one of the biggest parts of my education has been getting to know myself, finding out those things about myself that I like and things that I don't like. One of the most important parts of personal growth is learning to accept yourself.

Female: It's through other people that you really get to know yourself. It's also from the experiences you have and how you react to the experiences. I keep a journal, and I've been trying to write down a lot of what I feel about things that have happened to me or just things that have been going on.

Male: Knowing yourself is a process that never stops. It doesn't end in college. For the rest of your life, you'll be getting bits and pieces of everyone's opinion, an you're constantly influenced by the people around you. All of this is part of knowing yourself, liking yourself, and accepting yourself . . . then, you can begin to work on fulfilling yourself.

Summary

Students want college to be a place where they can discover themselves and realize mutually beneficial human relationships. They face a relatively uncertain future and perceive themselves to be on an adventure full of risk. As social and political issues lose their importance, personal development becomes the focus of care and concern. Will students become more flexible, responsive, creative, exuberant, and certain? They struggle with a dilemma of whether or not personal dreams can come true without an awareness of the plight of others and a sense of togetherness within a national or world community.

Part Two
Commentary

Students may move from activism to apathy, but their struggles to grow up are perennial. Helping students in this task is a challenge still not well met.

The Pains of Growing Up

Joseph Katz

Students Today

A superficial reading of what students said about themselves in the preceding chapters could leave one with the impression that we are dealing with a banal generation. Students seem to be preoccupied with themselves, concerned with their future material well-being, seduced into partying and endless talk in their residences. They seem to say little about the great ideas presented to them in their courses, not to speak of exhibiting a vigorous spirit of intellectual excitement and curiosity. Such a picture would not be unlike that which many of their professors have of their students as they perceive them in their classrooms. In some respects, it is even a true picture. At the same time, it is enormously false. Once one digs beneath the surface of what students say, one is confronted with at times poignant descriptions of their problems in growing up and the inadequate responses to them from teachers and other caretakers.

Separation from Home. The problems begin with the fact that college is no longer a voluntary choice. If one wants to make headway in the society, college attendance is compulsory. Having no choice is a challenge to young people who are wrestling with the problems of autonomy, who are struggling to be free from past dominations. Their bid for freedom is hampered by the compulsion of the next institutional step, and will be hampered once more when they enter the next corporation a few years hence.

For freshmen, in particular, the bid for independence involves a painful process of separation from home. They must give up the familiar sources of support, comfort, and affection that enveloped them in past years for the sake of making their way in the world. Once they leave home, they can never again expect support in the secure and generous ways their parents gave it.

Here ambiguities make the story even more complex. Home has not in all respects been supportive, a factor that has left its own wounds. There are at times poignant complaints of neglect or insufficient understanding. There may have been pressure to succeed and to live up to real or imagined expectations. For first-generation undergraduates, college threatens, for parents and children alike, to bring about estrangement from each other. Relations with mothers are more frequently reported as close than with fathers—a fact that may mirror their fathers' more frequent absence from the home. So they may enter the new adult world with a feeling of deficit and neglect that may be enhanced by the distance in faculty-student relationships. There are other conflicts engendered by the separation from home. Students comment that while at home they were taught virtues of honesty and cooperation. They report themselves driven by the academic situation into a self-centered competitiveness with other students, a manipulative orientation to teachers and making one's way, even an acceptance of cheating.

The pain of separation arises not only in regard to one's parents but also in regard to peers. Upon returning for the first visit home, the student may find that presumably lasting bonds have been loosened, at times to the point of indifference, and that, too, is part of the hardship of emotional leave-taking. The loss can be compensated for by the excitement of making new friends and discovering only partially known parts of the self through relationships with different people. But these new relationships and friendships are not themselves unencumbered. Again and again students say that they are unsure of themselves, that is, both unclear about what kind of people they are or want to be and doubting of their worth. Such lack of clarity and low self-esteem make it difficult, as some students perceive, to establish a relationship with another person. Because of the indefiniteness of self, one may be overly demanding or overly submissive, and both in turn.

Peers and Studying. The classroom, which could be one means of bringing people together around intellectual tasks, is almost universally reported not to be the place in which people get to know each other. The spatial proximity of many people in the dormitory at first can hide the soon only too apparent barriers due to clique, class, and ethnic differences. There are other disturbances in group living. Dormitories can be loud and noisy and hence interfere with study and the need for privacy. There can be peer pressure for partying, drinking, or drug taking. Many would like to resist but cannot muster the strength.

Students may not be putting in nearly the number of hours into their studies that their teachers want them to (and that they would need to put in to deal with their course subject matters more competently), but they feel that they have difficulty coping with the work. That difficulty may be due to inadequate preparation, competitiveness with others for grades, anxieties about the future if one does not do well, pressures from home to succeed, and lack of involvement in the content of many courses. Students often claim the apparent increase in drinking and alcoholism to be a response to such pressures. After a difficult test or by the time the weekend approaches, students feel that they can find relief in drinking.

There are other pressures. Greater sexual freedom has brought for at least some students the notion that they must perform sexually before they are really ready. Some students in a preceding chapter equated asking for a date with an invitation to go to bed together. One man went so far as to say that he felt a girl was hurt if after brief acquaintance he would not have sex with her. Moreover, if a relationship with a person of the opposite sex becomes more serious, the attempt to cope with the problems generated by intimacy— the more profound needs that people have of each other— begin to be a fresh source of anxiety if not depression.

The picture is a burdened one and may get more so. But my focus is on the problems and anxieties of students as they emerge from the data presented in the previous chapters. These problems are too often glossed over. Many of us need reminders that students are in varying degrees coping and even mastering these difficulties. There is a great sense of achievement and strength when that happens— and it could happen more often if we faced the reality of adolescents' struggles more clearly. Students learn, become more sophisticated, get to be more competent, and establish friendships. These experiences make the college years worthwhile, and the achievements are often better remembered than the pains that went with them, as unsolved problems may be shoved out of consciousness with time.

Much of what I have said thus far is more or less directly felt by the students themselves. Students would experience other matters as problems if they were able to attain a higher level of functioning. For example, they might recognize tensions between personal ambitions and identity and sense of community. A sense of community includes concern for the plight of others, a desire to do one's share to alleviate the suffering of others, to help them grow. Obstacles to community reside not only in competiveness and cliquishness, but also in alienating prejudices. Students wrestle with the problems of friendship, but they neglect not only their responsibility to the larger society outside of the college, but even to those among their college peers who seem to be uncomfortably different from them. There are ominous reports of the uglier forms of prejudice against other ethic groups and homosexuals to the point of degrading insults and abuse. There is affirmation of tolerance, but as the editors remark, such tolerance often is only verbal: problems are "weathered rather than resolved." Psychologically this means a continuing rigidity of attitude, an exclusion of emotional possibilities of warmth and understanding for others and, worse, a projection of what one condemns in oneself onto other people without any great clarity about the nature, sources, and relevance of the self-condemnation.

The College Environment. The spotlight thus far has been on the student's own emotional-intellectual state. But it is clear from what they say that the environment is an important contributing factor. They describe administrators as not listening to them. Academic advising often is considered a joke. Faculty-student separation is portrayed as a thick wall.

One issue highlights this alienation of student from faculty. Students say that academic dishonesty is widespread. What strikes some of them as particularly outrageous is that many teachers are indifferent when such dishonesty is being reported to them—something that students do with great difficulty because there is a strong feeling against telling on their peers. What explains such faculty indifference? For some teachers it may be an aversion to the role of policeman, avoidance of the cumbersome task of marshalling proof, or fear of the risk of making a false accusation. But perhaps the deeper reason is to save emotional and physical time. Faculty, for their part, are harassed people. In many institutions, they are besieged by demands for doing the kind of research and publications that will bring them promotion, tenure, and the respect of their peers. At the same time, their mobility has often diminished to near zero. Their status has declined, and their economic situation is in progressive decline—somewhat mitigated by the frequent involvement of their spouses in contributing to the family income. Greater numbers of students, different students, less well-prepared students, less submissive students than in the past, all have made the task of teaching more difficult. Hence, it seems that an implicit understanding has been established by which faculty gain more time for themselves by more sloppy attention to their classes, and students in turn try to manipulate their teachers toward easing the workload, for example, with shorter assignments, fewer tests. The grade inflation, now being somewhat reversed, is one such symptom. This situation of cutting corners at the expense of one's responsibilities as teachers and students is injurious to the integrity of both parties.

What Can Be Done?

Roles of Faculty and Student Affairs Educators. What can be done? It could be said that a concern for the psychological and moral well-being of students is not one that should be taken on by the college, that the institution is primarily addressed to academic education. That semirhetorical reply has lost some of its traditional power. It now emerges, and the pages in this book are testimony to it, that lack of integrity and motivation are having a clear influence on learning and academic performance. A kind of corruption has set in that affects both students and faculty in mutually reinforcing ways.

As far as the classroom and academic learning are concerned, perhaps the nub of the problem is a lack of attention to the specific learning capacities and ambitions of individual students and to the personalities in which curiosity and intellectual motivation are imbedded. Many professors view students primarily as fit objects for the cultivation or perpetuation of their specific scholarly or scientific subjects. There is little consideration of home background, preparation, values, aspirations, and personal dispositions. For instance, there is little exploration of the often severe problems of first-generation college students—of which we have so many. It is not only that new interests, attitudes, and ideologies pose a threat to one's ties with parents and the home community. Whatever their current academic attainments, at home and in high school these students may have been considered as "brains," and therefore also somewhat deviant. Their self-esteem is somewhat shakily based on their intellectual identity. Often professors, by implicitly or overtly considering these students as intellectually deficient, will undermine a major base of their security. Badmouthing of students is a not uncommon characteristic of faculty talk. The students sense it one way or the other. They get demoralized and they live out the negative expectations.

For faculty to get through to the many alienated and discouraged students in their classrooms, there seems to be no other way than acquiring better knowledge of their students. Much helpful literature is now available. But professors will build up relevant skills only through more systematic explorations of their students. Interviews of their students, individually or in groups, have been proven to work.

Recently there have been some very productive attempts in which faculty have taken the time during class periods to explore with their students the whats, hows, and whys of their learning in that particular course. Such inquiries have led to a different manner of presentation of subject matter and redefinition of curricular contents, particularly in introductory courses and courses for the nonmajor. But above all, they have alerted faculty to the learning dispositions, learning capacities, prior learning, and intellectual and personal styles of the specific students in front of them. The result is much improved communication and much greater pleasure of students and faculty in each other's presence—quite distinct from the pulling and evading that can characterize classrooms.

To move faculty in this direction will require more than the conventional efforts. Sometimes it is said that the reward structure needs to be changed and good teaching be recognized more fully. But this suggestion implies that faculty already know how to teach better, and only fail to use this knowledge for want of an incentive. It is more true to say that this knowledge still needs to be generated. In this task, student affairs professionals can render significant help. They can do so because, due to their training and the nature of their work, they have more multidimensional knowledge of student personalities and learning styles. They can help faculty to obtain a fuller picture of the students they face in their classrooms. But this possible cooperation of student affairs professionals and faculty would not be too productive were it confined to lecturing about student characteristics—one more indication of the instructional limits of the lecture. The best cooperation lies in student affairs professionals helping faculty to acquire the skills for getting to know their students better. They can provide training in interviewing and observing and how to use the information obtained by these means. A further dimension could be cooperation in the classroom in which faculty would be assisted in understanding such things as the group process in their classes or the nature and individual differences of student reactions to their teaching style.

Beyond that, because the classroom and the campus living community or student culture for the commuter student are so closely linked, attention to the one will also bring about changes in the other. Often the purposes of the classroom are defeated in the dormitory—for instance, because peer pressures, which many students would like to resist, draw energies and motivation away from studies and academic tasks. Here the student affairs professional can help by developing or using his or her knowledge of student peer pressure, tensions in interpersonal relationships, alienation, reliance on artificial means of stimulation and sedation. Too many institutions, by neglecting serious inquiry into student culture, undercut the potential rechanneling of psychological energies for the academic tasks of the college.

Student affairs divisions might adopt a more aggressive stance and make clear to administrators and faculty alike that they have information and skills that can serve the academic mission of the college centrally. Further, by linking students and faculty more closely with each other in and out of the classroom, student affairs professionals can help colleges to move towards that evanescent ideal of community. Faculty in turn can help by making it possible for students to have more intellectual self-respect—which comes through recognizing students in the contexts of their intellectual aspirations and capacities—thereby contributing to the students' growth in nonacademic areas. Intellectual self-esteem affects the self-concept and makes it easier to withstand peer pressures. It also, once pressure on self is released, makes it easier to pay empathic attention to other people.

What Students Can Do. The story often ends here. Improvement of the student situation is seen as a function of faculty or administration effort.

This view not only entails an exaggerated conception of faculty power, it contributes to absolving students from the very responsibility that is their developmental task. We need to confront our students more vigorously with what they contribute to the misunderstandings, frustrations, or boredom in their classrooms. They fail to perceive much good teaching because of a passive reliance on professors doing more than their share. But learning largely is self-learning. This simple truth has been obscured because administrators and even faculty now often tend to view students as paying customers who need to be pleased. Moreover, the increased sophistication about student developmental patterns (for example, Perry or Piaget) has seemed to demand even more initiative of the teacher. Some faculty seem to think that if they only knew the right cognitive buttons to press, their students would shortly turn into mature and committed reasoners or articulate writers.

The real challenge consists of exploring with students the obstacles they may face in any particular course. This of course becomes a two-way street because faculty will have to be willing to adapt their challenges to the students' capacities. Even knowledge of capacities is not enough; for good learning will take place only if the student's motivations and incentives are also engaged. This need not, and should not, entail catering to whatever tendencies students might have to shun the harder tasks. But teachers cannot challenge students, as they now so often do, in the abstract. A new cooperation between professors and students is needed that encourages joint analysis as often as necessary about the methods and substance of a course and the students' responses to the tasks set before them. This will inevitably lead teachers to change, sometimes substantially, what they teach, as well as the methods they use to facilitate learning.

It is not uncommon to have teachers address themselves conscientiously to specific tasks, such as trying to teach their students to write better or to induce them to think more independently. Often they report success with some students, failure with others. There the matter usually rests. I am proposing turning away from such "hit and miss" efforts and instead proceeding—with the cooperation of the students concerned—to an analysis of the misses. If teachers subjected their teaching to continuous reflective inquiries, students might become more reflective about their learning. In my own experience, having two professors cooperate on the tasks of analyzing teaching and learning has been particularly productive. I am speaking not of team teaching but of having a colleague serve, on a more or less regular basis through a semester or year, as a nonteaching observer. Interviews of students about *how* they learn can be very useful. Interviews of an entire class by a faculty observer, in the presence of their teacher, have also turned out to be very revealing and thought-provoking.

Beyond the classroom, faculty and student affairs professionals alike might engage students in reflections that would aim at increasing considerably the awareness and self-questioning of students in regard to why they are in college, what they want to accomplish there, how their present actions and thinking contribute to making them the kind of people they are, and what potential for growth and happy achievement is vitiated by their present behavior. All these efforts center on having students become more active and deliberate in the pursuit of what is good for them. This includes their perceiving more vividly the larger contexts of the society and the world on which they depend for security and for the enlargements of their provincial selves. There is, with all the pain that I have described, a heavy gloss of triviality in current students' lives. It is much in their own self-interest to rouse themselves beyond it.

Joseph Katz is chairperson of the Group for Human Development and Educational Policy of the State University of New York at Stony Brook. Since 1961 he has studied the intellectual and emotional development of college students in many different institutions. He always works on the translation of research into educational practice.

Although many postsecondary education institutions reinforce the feelings of students that they are powerless and encourage them to be passive citizens, a new breed of student activists is seeking resources to build sophisticated networks and advocacy organizations on the local, state, and national levels.

Majoring in Self-Interest, Minoring in Apathy: A Challenge for the New Activists

Kathleen M. Downey

Through their intensive study of college student behavior and attitudes, DeCoster and Mable have reached some disturbing, and in my judgment, accurate conclusions about the social and political attitudes of today's college students. According to their findings, students are most concerned about personal goals such as maintaining a high grade point average, developing their personality, having fun, and eventually finding high-paying employment. Unlike their predecessors in the sixties, they show little interest in addressing political and social injustices and instead frequently ally themselves with individuals who they perceive to have power and influence, the "establishment" itself. Some students hope that knowing or being in with these powerful persons will bring a future payoff in the form of recommendations, references, or direct assistance in their quest for future employment.

DeCoster and Mable also discovered more revealing facts about the personal feelings of students, which provides a better understanding of why they have selected individual priorities over the concerns of society as a whole. For the most part, students feel that they are powerless, ineffective, and isolated from the real world and that the leadership of their peers is

D. A. DeCoster and P. Mable (Eds.), *New Directions for Student Services: Understanding Today's Students,* no. 16. San Francisco: Jossey Bass, 1981.

unimportant and not deserving of respect. Such conclusions are very distressing since many of these individuals will be tomorrow's leaders.

Through this commentary, I will attempt to explain events and experiences that have helped students to form these views, describe the forces on campus that perpetuate these unhealthy attitudes, and discuss positive steps taken by individual students and student organizations to reverse an apathetic, me-oriented trend.

Factors Contributing to Social and Political Apathy

In order to fully understand the apathetic and individualistic views of today's students, one must carefully examine two major factors: (1) the turbulent times of their childhood and (2) the competitive educational system in which they participated for so many years.

First, let us review the politically unstable and turbulent times that comprised the childhood years of today's college students. The most publicized national event, which took place in the first years of their lives, was the assassination of President John F. Kennedy. This murder was followed by the senseless killing of two other prominent leaders, Robert F. Kennedy and Martin Luther King, Jr. All three of these men were considered to be movers and shakers. To many, their assassinations illustrated vividly that individuals who challenge the status quo do so at great risk with the possibility of violent retaliation. Today, nearly twenty years after the first assassination, we still have no real closure regarding these murders. Countless books and articles have been written concerning various theories and conspiracies, particularly about John Kennedy, linking high government officials and agencies in a plot.

These growing years were also marred by the war in Vietnam, which touched the lives of so many of today's students and split the country. Throughout their childhood, they witnessed the death of family and friends of other young American men and women, and of the people of Vietnam. The destruction of the villages and homes of an impoverished people— documented daily through television coverage—continued like an ongoing soap opera. In the end, the wisdom of many political and military leaders was discredited, and the war, which ended without resolution, was quickly removed from public view and forgotten.

For many, Watergate was the final blow. It either confirmed the cynical belief that politicians were crooked and have always been playing dirty tricks or smashed the optimistic view that lawmakers are really honorable people. Those who had not formed an opinion prior to Watergate became very cynical and wary of the political system. Even the message from the youngest person entangled in the Watergate scandal to other young people considering a political career was to stay away. Many young people resigned themselves to the fact that most politicians either began or would end their careers as self-serving, dishonest individuals.

Since citizens are virtually powerless to prevent political corruption, actively supporting and voting for such individuals simply did not make sense.

Arthur Levine, a senior fellow at the Carnegie Foundation for the Advancement of Teaching, confirmed the fact that Vietnam and Watergate had a profound effect on the attitude of today's college students. In his well-researched book entitled *When Dreams and Heroes Died* (1981), Levine noted that students linked Watergate and the Vietnam War as corrupt events that are indigenous to our political system. Students have readily accepted the fact that political leaders are corrupt and their behavior is represented in all sectors of society, including large corporations and organized religion.

Second, today's college students were educated in a fiercely competitive and individualistic educational system. Throughout elementary and secondary school, students were encouraged to compete for grades, honors, and the teacher's approval. Frequent contests were conducted teaming the boys against the girls and one half of the room against the other. As a child, it was vitally important to overcome the opponents and win.

On the whole, students were encouraged to be concerned about their own academic advancement and achievements while being discouraged from working with and helping others. In some instances, the brighter students were asked to assist those having difficulty—a cooperative learning environment that was certainly not the norm. Dividing students into track systems by praising the successful and humiliating the less gifted was a simpler solution.

Elementary and secondary school also became the training ground for learning how to run the maze, where clever students quickly realized how to play the game. Those who agreed with the teachers and regurgitated their beliefs would be rewarded with good grades. Nonconformists and those who asked too many questions were labeled as troublemakers, given lower grades, and provided with demerits or detention.

Conditions Perpetuating Student Apathy

Once students leave high school and enter college, the situation does not improve. Even though college is supposed to be a time for learning and expanding horizons through new experiences, these institutions reinforce the feelings of students that they are powerless and isolated and that their peers serving in leadership positions are ineffective. In addition, many higher education institutions encourage students to become passive citizens agreeing to the social priorities and social norms constructed by lawmakers. Well-known consumer advocate, Ralph Nader (1979), summarized this role of colleges and universities in his article, "Student Power 101," which appeared in *Change Magazine*.

> It is widely assumed to academics that the business of education is the fuller development of each new generation. I suggest that there is

enough evidence to show that this assumption is often based on academic myths and not on facts. Even with the proliferation of degree-holding young people over the past twenty years, there has not been a corresponding increase in the number of social innovators developing or applying the analyses and solutions to our nation's common problems. Instead, what America has seen—in what has become a litany of misdeeds—is a parade of all too many highly trained, well-educated people using their skills and their training to circumvent solutions, to avoid complying with laws, or to devise intricate patterns of corruption.... Why, then, aren't the universities educating large numbers of people to work actively as citizens to solve some of these social ills? The question immediately arises: Do curriculum—and the qualities that universities reward—discourage responsible citizenship while encouraging a straight-line, get-ahead career and life-style? (p. 47)

Few, if any, steps are being taken to correct the negative reinforcement of colleges and universities. It is difficult to foresee positive changes until students fully realize that they are attending dictatorial institutions that are not training them to resolve critical social problems or to cherish a democratic system.

Thus, two major conditions perpetuate the problems of student apathy and self-centeredness: (1) decision-making authority is typically placed in the hands of a few campus administrators and (2) student governing bodies are deliberately designed for failure.

The Concentration of Administrative Power

Except in rare instances, complete decision-making authority rests in the hands of a few administrators who have no defined role of accountability to students. For the most part, public university systems are ultimately governed by a statewide body called the Board of Regents, while independent schools are led by a local body called the Board of Trustees. In both instances, the selection process for board members is based on political motives, and individuals are selected for their well-publicized names, political influence, wealth, or connections to the business sector. Needless to say, students do not generally meet these criteria, and unless specifically required by law, students are not invited to participate on governing boards.

In fact, a study completed by the Association of Governing Boards of Colleges and Universities (AGB) (1977) found that students comprise only 1 percent of all college governing boards. These boards are provided with staff and financial resources, and they are also entrusted with the responsibility to determine policies and shape the direction of higher education institutions. Yet for the most part, board members are totally removed from the everyday world where students live and learn. This same report indicated that most board members have not attended college in nearly thirty years, as two of every three trustees are fifty years of age or older. Women, who comprise the majority of the college population, and minorities, which make up an increasing number of college enrollments, are inadequately represented: only 15 percent and 7 precent of governing board members are women or minorities, respectively.

In addition, members of college and university governing bodies are not informed about student attitudes and do not advocate the expressed concerns of students on such issues as rising tuition and dwindling financial aid. A recent article in *The Chronicle of Higher Education* (1981), confirmed this fact. When a reporter attended the annual AGB conference, he found that members of the college and university governing boards were not willing to become involved in the political struggles resulting from President Reagan's proposed budget cuts. While board members include some of the country's most influential citizens, they are either unwilling or unprepared to accept any major lobbying or advocacy role on behalf of postsecondary education. Rationalizations are commonplace: "It's very dangerous for a trustee to discuss things in public. He could be misquoted or he might contradict the views of other board members." Another favorite maneuver is to pass the responsibility for public comment to the administration: "The owners of the ship hire the captain to run it" (Jacobson, 1981, p. 6).

Meanwhile on the campus level, most policies affecting students are determined by the student activities or student life office. These offices are staffed by middle managers who usually report to a dean of students or vice-president for student affairs who, in turn, answers to the college president. Working closely with students and providing them with decision-making capacities is completely optional for these individuals. On the whole, students and student organizations have found that campus administrators are reluctant to share their powers or to allow alternative views presented by students to be given equal consideration.

Administrators, unfortunately, find it expedient to dominate the decision-making process on college campuses, ignoring the fact that these institutions exist for students as educational consumers. This domination continues because college administrators have distinct advantages and resources that allow them to retain power:
- full-time salaries
- professional legitimacy
- support staff
- professional organizations
- formal and specialized training
- independent funding bases
- access to equipment, supplies, and other resources

- continuity and experience
- time to devote the educational issues as a part of their paid responsibility.

In contrast, students do not possess these resources, and their situation can be characterized quite differently:
- minimal or no compensation for participation in student activities through academic credit or salary
- little or no support staff
- inadequate or no formalized training
- limited professional legitimacy, because student associations are reduced to club status with no real decision-making authority
- limited control over student activity fees.

When students seriously attempt to become participants in governance many administrators use their power and influence to co-opt them. Administrators often create the illusion that they believe in student representation and power by recognizing the student leaders as "special individuals" They do so by confiding allegedly privileged information, allowing them to assist in running student services, giving them preference in selecting class schedules, and distributing free tickets to campus cultural and sporting events. They do not, however, allow students to develop the institutional budget and program priorities, nor do they support even token, much less equal, representation on decision-making bodies. Student leaders often "take the bait" and begin to think that they are achieving status by receiving these special favors. They begin to identify with the administrators and support their positions, and they quickly understand that it is personally more rewarding to take advantage of the special treatment and favors posed by administrators than to struggle to make administrators more responsive.

One of two things typically happens to student leaders who refuse to become co-opted. Either administrators will respect them for having the courage of their convictions, or the administrators will convince faculty, students, and other policy makers that these leaders are crazies or radicals and reduce their effectiveness, describing them as arrogant, ungrateful, or immature.

Student Governing Bodies Are Designed for Failure

The traditional model for student representation on most college and university campuses is a student government association (SGA). Most SGA members are elected by the small percentage of the campus population who decide to cast a vote. In some isolated instances, student government associations have been able to effectively represent the interests and concerns of the students. In the majority of cases, the student government is not very effective because it has been designed to fail. Student governments:

- have no real decision-making authority
- lack continuity and cohesiveness
- have no mentors or even committed advisors and advocates
- have no formalized training.

As previously stated, college administrators are reluctant to share their power with students. As a result, student government representatives are not given any of the real decision-making capabilities that will determine the future of the college. Instead, they are forced to grapple with such trivia as pep rallies, homecoming parades, campus political squabbles, and attacks on individual student government members. Sometimes they are graced with decisions that will either divide the student body or the SGA. As long as students are fighting among themselves, they will not have the time and energy to question the administration.

One of the most serious limitations of student government associations is the lack of continuity resulting from a high turnover rate in both the constituencies and leadership of student organizations. The leader of student groups find themselves becoming involved in the organization; gaining experience, perspective, and judgment; moving up through the ranks; and upon reaching some level of effectiveness they graduate. The cycle must begin again, usually without any transition of experience, guidance, and written materials to allow the next group of student leaders to complete or follow-up the projects of their predecessors.

Central to this problem of a lack of continuity are the lack of student mentors and formalized training. Unlike administrators, new members of a student government rarely have an individual or individuals with experience, know-how, and a student advocacy perspective who will help them begin their term. Usually no one on campus is available to reinforce positive actions of the student government leaders. Often students need to be told when they are doing a good job and that their concern about their education and the future direction of society is responsible behavior. The University of Massachusetts at Amherst is one of the few campuses where mentors are available to provide support to student leaders. Through their Student Center for Educational Research and Advocacy, Amherst students have access to full-time staff members who assist student leaders in coordinating activities dealing with student rights, tenant rights, women and minority rights, academic affairs, and student services. This center is totally governed and funded by students.

Students also need training from their mentors or from an outside group. Without sophisticated skills, these novice student leaders cannot begin to negotiate and compete successfully with highly experienced and trained administrators. Student government leaders need, yet rarely receive, training in the following areas:

- analyzing the power structure on campus and its relation to society

- determining how to work with the power structure and make it more responsive
- designing strategies to bring about desired change
- evaluating the effectiveness of their programs.

Students Can Facilitate Change

Students, like most special-interest groups, support national advocacy organizations that represent their interests and concerns in Washington, D.C. The National Student Association (NSA) was formed for this purpose in 1947. NSA championed issues such as civil rights, student participation in governance, and educational and social reform. In 1972 the National Student Lobby (NSL) was formed to address a concern of some student leaders that NSA was not lobbying enough on student issues. At the same time, the National Student Educational Fund (NSEF) was founded to serve as the research and development arm of the Student Lobby. NSEF worked primarily on issues such as student consumer rights and financial aid information.

In 1978, the NSA and NSL joined forces to become the most powerful national student membership association in the country. The name of the newly merged organization is the United States Student Association (USSA). At present USSA and NSEF work closely together on matters of mutual concern to complete projects that will build a strong, grassroots network of students across the country. This work is being completed through information dissemination and organizing projects targeting state student associations, women's organizations, minority groups, student peer counselors, and student government associations, as well as other national organizations.

State Student Associations

Within the past decade, a new and innovative form of student representation has emerged to meet the challenges facing higher education and society. Student voices are being heard through the development of state and system student associations, better known as SSAs. These organizations can best be described as multicampus coalitions whose aim is to influence local, state, and federal officials as well as educational policy makers.

The impetus for the establishment of these organizations grew from three major situations. First, students realized that the traditional student government model of representation was ineffective. If their opinions were to be heard, students were in need of an office in the state capital staffed by full-time advocates who could provide them with needed information, representation, and training. Second was the realization that higher education was no longer a funding priority in many state legislatures. Third, students realized that higher education was becoming more complex in its structure and that decisions were increasingly being made by professionals, particularly in the state capitals, removed from the campuses.

SSAs have commanded much respect and attention. An article appearing in *The Chronicle of Higher Education* (1978) noted that their efforts represented a new and significant trend in student politics. Legislators and educators in several states believed that these organizations were generally well respected and had great potential. They used such words as "legitimate," "effective," and "discipline" in describing these associations.

The primary concern of SSAs has been to ensure high-quality, low-cost higher education to their constituents. This goal has been accomplished through a variety of ways such as ongoing student and staff lobbying, rallies, letter-writing campaigns, and marches, coupled with voter registration and political education drives.

Interest in tuition issues is not the only concern of SSAs. Overall, they have served as effective student advocates on a statewide and campus level by attempting to improve the quality of education. This has been accomplished through student involvement in the student consumer movement in such activities as: ensuring due process through the grievance procedure system; improving campus health care, counseling, childcare, and financial aid services; clarifying tenants' rights; placing students on boards of trustees, financial aid advisory committees, and statewide planning commissions; eliminating discrimination; and monitoring truth in advertising in student handbooks and catalogs.

As the primary mission of maintaining high-quality, low-cost education and other accompanying student consumer concerns becomes institutionalized in the everyday operations of the SSA, these organizations are beginning to take a more active role in addressing social concerns of their members. Unfortunately, the role of the students in providing information and organizing support for a wide variety of progressive causes on the public agenda has not been publicized by the press. Statewide student groups in Pennsylvania, New York, California, and Wisconsin have addressed issues of racism, sexism, arms build-up and registration for the draft.

At present, 100 state student associations exist across the country in nearly every state and the District of Columbia. Many of these, however, consist of no more than a collection of student government leaders on individual campuses with no staff, experience, or formal statewide status. Twenty-four states have at least one half-time member, yet only eleven within the states of California (two), Pennsylvania, New York (two), Kansas, Missouri, Wisconsin, Oregon, Arizona, and Florida have reached maturity with full-time directors, state capital lobbyists, an office, and stable budgets.

In every case, it has been the more stable and developed state student associations that have been the most successful in overcoming the problems of traditional student governments, because they have full-time staff to bridge the continuity gap and adequate budgets to provide them with greater resources and legitimacy. Within the past year, both NSEF and USSA have witnessed a growing interest on the part of student leaders to build successful statewide groups that will effectively represent the interests of the college students.

The National Student Educational Fund has also discovered that individual students and campus student organizations are identifying problems and designing solutions. For three years, NSEF sponsored a mini-grant program and a better information contest. Through these projects, NSEF was able to identify over 500 student-initiated projects designed to help their peers. Some of these projects include:

- braille campus maps for blind students
- handbooks outlining off-campus shops, restaurants, movie theaters, and so on that could accommodate persons in a wheelchair
- survival guides
- financial aid handbooks
- guides for women returning to school after many years
- faculty evaluations
- actions to make minority students on a predominantly white campus feel more comfortable.

The National Student Educational Fund and the United States Student Association are trying to build a grass-roots student movement that will alter our inhuman, competitive educational system with the firm conviction that individual students do have the power to make a difference. They teach students to identify problems, analyze their origins, develop solutions, implement those solutions, and evaluate their effectiveness.

Many of today's college students want to change the educational and social system but need the confidence and information to participate in such a movement. Thus, student leaders are optimistic that national student groups in conjunction with other local, statewide, and national organizations concerned about social injustices will begin to demand more from educational and political policy makers. Such partnerships, coalitions, and mutual understanding will begin to transform the role of campus student governance from its present floundering status to a position of respect, responsibility, and effective use of legitimate decision-making power. Students as citizens and consumers must develop, maintain, and protect their individual and collective rights, as well as responsibilities to contribute to their own educational experience.

Despite the negative reports concerning the social and political attitudes of students as noted by DeCoster, Mable, Levine, and others, I am optimistic. I am optimistic because student activists have overcome incredible odds to seek resources to build sophisticated networks and advocacy organizations on the local, state, and national level. These activists have been able to acquire excellent lobbying, organizing, and management skills despite countless roadblocks that have deliberately been placed in their path by other members of the higher education community. By receiving additional assistance from the national student groups and each other, student advocacy organizations will be able to overcome roadblocks with greater ease and at the same time increase their visibility, credibility, and influence. In turn, these student advocates are motivating their peers and providing them with a sense of purpose by illustrating how the political system affects their daily lives, including their education; encouraging them to participate and influence the political system by campaigning and voting; and informing them about the social and economic inequities that negatively affect many Americans.

Summary

The 1980s will be a crucial decade for the future of the higher education system. Its financing, credibility, and value have been placed on the firing line. If higher education is to regain its reputation and esteem, the system must begin to train innovators who will honestly attempt to resolve our nation's complex social and economic problems rather than to contribute to them. It must also help to form an electorate that will force lawmakers to be accountable to the entire public as opposed to a select few with wealth and prestige. Higher education can meet these goals by providing students with a training ground that allows them to join educators and lawmakers in determining policy.

References

Association of Governing Boards of Colleges and Universities. *Higher Education Panel Report No. 35*. Washington, D.C.: Association of Governing Boards of Colleges and Universities, 1977.
Jacobson, R. L. "Despite Budgeting Crises, College Trustees Are Reluctant Lobbyists." *The Chronicle of Higher Education*, April 13, 1981, p. 6.
Jacobson, R. L. "Students Seek New Clout Through Statewide Coalitions." *The Chronicle of Higher Education*, November 13, 1978, pp. 7–8.
Levine, A. *When Dreams and Heroes Died: A Portrait of Today's College Student*. San Francisco: Jossey-Bass, 1980.
Nader, R. "Student Power 101." *Change Magazine,* 1979, *11* (8), 47–50.

Kathleen M. Downey is the president of the National Student Educational Fund, a Washington-based organization that provides technical assistance to campus and statewide student organizations. Before joining NSEF in 1979, she served as the executive director of the Commonwealth Association of Students in Pennsylvania for two years. She is a graduate of West Chester State College in Pennsylvania.

Satisfactions and dissatisfactions of students in postsecondary institutions should challenge administrators to be visionary and assertive in managing the educational enterprise for human development.

Facilitating Human Development Through Administrative Leadership

Milton E. Wilson

Administrators in postsecondary education are to serve the educational community by facilitating the educational process and by creating and maintaining an environment conducive to teaching, research, and service. Student expressions of satisfaction and dissatisfaction with the educational processes and milieu, offer insights into administrative effectiveness in assessing student needs and in planning, organizing, facilitating, and evaluating services and opportunities for meeting them. Such insights can challenge administrators to actively respond to the needs of students and institutions for more effective transactions and ways to realize the educational mission.

Because administrators formulate policy, implement services, and manage organizations that deliver opportunities relevant to the educational mission of the institution, feedback from students on the effects of these efforts is critical in the planning, organizing, allocating, and evaluative responsibilities of administrators.

The purposes of this commentary are to ferret out some of the major insights articulated by students in the evaluation of their educational experiences, examine the corresponding administrative implications, and put forth a challenge for visionary and assertive leadership that will result in greater student development.

D. A. DeCoster and P. Mable (Eds.), *New Directions for Student Services: Understanding Today's Students,* no. 16. San Francisco: Jossey Bass, 1981.

What Students Tell Us About Their Educational Experiences

The primary obligation of postsecondary education is to maximize human development for the benefit of individual students and the society in which they must function. To realize this obligation, institutions must influence the developmental activities of students by providing the academic atmosphere, the human associations, and the discipline vital to the student's sound intellectual growth and character development. Both curricular and extracurricular activities are designed to stimulate curiosity, broaden perspective, enrich awareness, deepen understanding, establish disciplined habits of thought, provide vocational skills, and help students realize their potentials as responsible and informed members of society. As indicated in the earlier chapters, while emphasis may vary from time to time, place to place, and group to group, these goals remain fundamentally similar.

Student Satisfactions and Dissatisfactions. While embracing the traditional goals, students report both satisfactions and dissatisfactions with their educational experiences. Among the satisfactions expressed are: broadened perspective, enriched awareness, increased understanding, preparation for a vocation, activities, peer support and friendship, and family relationships. But students also express a good deal of dissatisfaction or frustration with regard to:

- orientation to institutions and their expectations
- faculty-student advising, contact, and transactions
- multicultural understanding and appreciation; skills in relating to foreign, minority, handicapped, and older students, and to persons who have different religious or sexual preference orientations
- ethical issues and values related to abuse of alcohol and drugs; sexuality; living environments; academic honesty, integrity, and standards
- political and citizenship issues, including leadership, student government, and assertive citizenship behaviors
- bureaucracy and genuine commitment to understanding students and to a student development perspective among administrators and faculty.

It seems quite clear that students are cognizant of the roles they are to play as productive workers, and they are concerned about their vocational development, their career choices, and the roads to career success. They are less encouraged and less involved, however, in the kinds of activities that help them become effective and participating citizens. It seems, therefore, that postsecondary institutions as a whole need to provide the means for students to become productive citizens as well as productive workers. Career productivity occurs after all within a citizenship role. Students can be motivated to prepare for that enlarged role through student government, multicultural activities, and other kinds of involvement that would help them understand, think about, and deal effectively with local, national, or international issues.

Attaining Educational Goals. While positive outcomes like personal and career development may result from the postsecondary educational experience, some desirable goals are never realized. Students may leave college without understanding individuals from other cultural backgrounds, may be unable to form adequate relationships, or may fail to take initiative in citizenship and leadership roles. Possibly these goals have never been realized because effective models of student development have not been available. In addition, students' interactions with other students, faculty, and community as well as the institutional policies, incentives, rules, and regulations may facilitate or hinder student development.

Student Interactions with the Educational Environment. Just as behavior is a function of the interaction of the person with the environment, student development is a function of the interaction of the student with the educational environment—faculty, friends, books, policies, grades, and so forth.

While student background differences may help or hinder the realization of educational outcomes, faculty, staff, and student attitudes and behaviors at times are not congruent with developmental objectives, unless part of the educational process is learning to deal effectively with ambiguity, conflicting notions, and confrontive negotiations.

When goals are not attained, it is worthwhile to look at problems regarding the abilities of the students and the environment but also to look at the quality and quantity of student interactions with the environment.

Administrative and Managerial Implications

The satisfactions and dissatisfactions of students are in part related to variable administrative skills in clarifying and articulating the educational mission and objectives. What follows is a brief discussion of several challenges relevant to administrative and managerial effectiveness in postsecondary education.

Close the Gap Between Promises and Outcomes. Many promises are implied in the postsecondary educational experience. While some of the promises are achieved, many are not. With respect to goals, objectives, and methods, institutions must say what they mean and mean what they say. Articulating the truth in educational advertising is one of our major challenges. While the realization of some goals may be frustrated by deficits in students, others may be frustrated by deficits in the institution. In either case, the transactions between students and their environments do not lead to the realization of the desired outcomes. Greater specificity and monitoring of educational objectives, criteria, and methods are needed to close the "effectiveness" gap. Thus, operational definitions of mission and objective statements are important. Developing student capabilities to cope with privations and frustrations in earlier educational experiences, can maximize the possibilities for realizing desired cognitive and affective outcomes.

Certainly, the access of minorities, the handicapped, older, and foreign students to postsecondary institutions presents opportunities for the development of human relations and cross-cultural understandings and skills. But these outcomes will not be realized without facilitative planning, organization, and skilled utilization of resources and interactions. In a large sense, what happens to culturally different, disadvantaged, handicapped, foreign, and minority students on campuses is a barometer of the validity and strength of educational systems. When these systems become more viable for these groups, they will become better systems for all groups.

Question and Test Assumptions About Students. Because of student diversity, research and evaluation are important to administrative and managerial effectiveness. We cannot really say that we know or understand students until we receive verification of our understanding through their feedback. Indeed, students are asking: "Is anyone listening?" And in controversies, they are saying: "You really don't know me," "You misunderstood what I said," and "Please understand where my head is and where I am coming from."

Moreover, not all students of any group have all the characteristics attributed to that group, and no characteristic is typical of every student of any one group or of no other group. There is a wide range of physical and mental abilities and talent among students of every group, and no group is inherently superior to any other.

Because of the heterogeneity of today's students, we dare not assume too much about anything without appropriate assessment—especially preparation for academic work, congruence of value orientations with the traditional priorities of the institution, readiness to profit from multicultural contacts, and participation in citizenship challenges. We need to know where individuals are in terms of the cognitive and affective characteristics they bring to the educational setting.

The same considerations also hold for other constituent groups— faculty, staff, parents, and citizens. We must learn the importance of describing subgroups and how they are interrelated and contribute to or detract from the effectiveness of the institution. Moreover, we need to check on the potency of the institution and its policies, programs, and services for fostering educational development. We must not assume without evidence that policies, programs, staff, and transactions are satisfactory or facilitative. We must ask: "How do we know?" "What is the evidence?" We must understand the sense of community and the extent and quality of communication among members of the community. Policies, programs, and staff must receive reviews that communicate satisfaction, dissatisfaction, and necessary modifications. We must learn the differences between the expectations and the realities of the institutions for community members, how these discrepancies are adjusted, and how the adjustments facilitate the realization of the educational mission.

In addition, we must not assume that we have been successful in identifying and meeting all the needs for students or for programming potency. Unmet and unarticulated needs may exist, and we must constantly monitor students and environments in terms of needs assessment. This is particularly true today because broadened access has brought about changes in the student body. Along with the traditional young adult who matriculates from high school with an appropriate preparatory background, two major groups with special needs, especially the need for flexibility, have arrived on campuses. Cross (1980b) refers to these two groups as new students and nontraditional students, and she argues that "Present concerns about quality reflect the considerable problems of traditional educational structures attempting to cope with escalating student diversity" (p. 14).

Focus on the Student and Student Development. Any policy, program, or person that frustrates or diminishes student development is not congruent with the mission of postsecondary education. The student and his or her development are central to achieving desired educational outcomes.

While student development objectives exist, and for the most part are fairly well accepted despite the varied development language, they are seldom defined operationally. Thus, the assessment of student development outcomes leaves much to be desired. Indeed, every institutional message should be articulated and evaluated in terms of the centrality of students and their development. Every role should be analyzed for this emphasis. There should be no doubt about the answers to the questions: Why does the institution exist? Why are we here? What are we doing?

Moreover, curricular and extracurricular programmatic efforts should center around students and their needs rather than administrative convenience or existing resources. A commitment is needed toward discovering new ways of providing opportunities, new combinations of services, and new kinds of both services and opportunities to meet the needs of students.

We should ask: What are we doing? Why are we doing it? Does it make a difference? All of the answers should point to our contributions to student enrollment, retention, well-being, and development. Particular attention should be given to the fostering and development of participatory and leadership skills, management of time and stress, development of moral perspectives, and knowledge of human relations, attitudes, and skills.

Students' testimonies in news columns and yearbooks emphasize that student development is holistic. Student development is the synergistic expression of curricular and extracurricular experience, which we must help students synthesize and assess in terms of achieving their own educational objectives.

Improve Human Relationships. Relationships that influence educational development require examination and, in almost every case, improvement. These include relationships among faculty and students, administrators and parents, parents and students, and multicultural relationships (transethnic, cross-cultural, cross-age, and cross-ability). Facilitative contact among individuals must be fostered. Acceptance of the importance and value of diversity must be reinforced along with the acknowledgment that differences do not denote inferiority or superiority.

The university needs to recognize that interpersonal skills, participation in groups, thinking rationally and objectively about people, relating to others with positive emotion, and the art of problem solving are vital to educational experiences. The importance of citizenship development and the assessment of problem solving related to social and political problems also require emphasis, for the decency of American society depends upon the caring of citizens and their willingness and commitment to engage in problem-solving processes.

Accept Educational Responsibilities. Faculty, administrators, staff, and students have responsibilities as well as rights in the educational enterprise, and these responsibilities should be identified, articulated, modeled, reinforced, and evaluated. At the heart of the ethical responsibilities of faculty, administrators, and students is the recognition that the building and practice of mutual respect must be the basis for interactions valuing interdependence and the modeling of responsible behaviors. Students must understand and reinforce their rights and responsibilities. They must also realize that discipline is part of the academic and extracurricular experience.

Citizenship responsibilities and standards should also be articulated and promoted. Citizens are a group of people who share a common good, regard the community as their own, and are held personally responsible for acts that harm or benefit the common good of the community. Motivating faculty, staff, and students to be good citizens and to exercise their rights and responsibilities in the educational community, as well as in the larger society, promotes the acceptance of diversity of culture and style as a basic good.

Create Viable Interdependencies. Educational goals and objectives cannot be realized without viable interdependence among the persons and agencies in the educational enterprise. Viable interdependencies are characterized by common goals, mutuality of respect, and the necessity for cooperative action. Interdependence, cooperation, and synergism all refer to cooperative actions of separate elements—like academic affairs and student affairs—that together have greater total impact upon student development and satisfaction than the sum of the individual effects.

Within and among departments and units in academic affairs, student affairs, and business affairs, interdependencies should be recognized and fostered. While the interdependencies exist among these units, their effectiveness is variable and sometimes unrecognized until crises and conflicts occur. Conflicts in interdependencies are inevitable, but they have the potential for producing highly constructive consequences. Confrontation can be desirable when the overall social context is predominantly cooperative, when norms and values support conflict management, and when the disagreeing parties have the skills, attitudes, and strategies to manage such situations positively.

Involvement, motivation, understanding, learning, and the resolution of controversy (disagreement among ideas, opinions, theories, methods, and conclusions) are all closely related. Properly managed, controversy encourages inquiry, promotes objectivity, sharpens analysis, promotes the search for new and better alternatives, and motivates imaginative and productive synthesis.

Therefore, mechanisms for expressing and resolving problems, conflicts, and grievances should be clearly understood and utilized. This includes mechanisms for student conduct violations and conflicts regarding cheating and plagiarism, substance abuse, and living conditions believed to compromise safety, quiet, cleanliness, and so forth.

In addition, conflicts and controversies in the workplace must be monitored and resolved. The workplace must be conducive to teaching, learning, student development, research, inquiry, and service. Positive impacts in the environment in which educational interactions occur should result from administrative planning, organizing, controlling, directing, and evaluating.

We must collaborate to improve coordination through problem solving. People who recognize their interdependence and seek common goals must clarify their roles, carry out joint planning and problem solving, and become more self-analytic and effective in their work with each other. The perception of equal status of persons in realizing goals is important, and the devaluation of others cannot be tolerated. Accessibility, willingness to communicate honestly, feedback, and two-way communication are also crucial.

The Call for Visionary Leadership

Visionary leadership is essential to bring out the best in faculty, staff, and students; to support the mission of postsecondary education; and to reconcile, transcend, and synergize self-interests. Visionary leadership inspires emulation, purposiveness, and problem solving. It also balances concern for people with concern for the mission and improves the workplace and the work force through increased levels of trust and teamwork. While visionary leadership may not produce immediate and dramatic change, it marshals resources to move in the desired direction.

Cross (1980a) has pointed to the challenge for visionary leadership among student personnel administrators, especially assertive leadership in articulating and achieving the most productive transactions between learners and providers: "Educational consumers have never possessed more clout, nor have educational providers ever been more responsive to the desires of what is blatantly called 'the market'. Both are seeking the link that will bring them together. Learners want to know how they can best meet their needs, and providers want to be responsive. The student personnel profession has an unprecedented opportunity in these formative years of the learning society to provide the linking service that will bring learners and providers together in the most productive combinations. No role is more important in the development of the learning society, and no profession is better suited to helping people of all ages and from all walks of life request and select the kind of education that will enhance the quality of their lives" (p. 104).

Silverman (1980) also has put forth the argument that student personnel administrators are in a key position to maximize the realization of the mission of postsecondary education. He argues that student personnel administrators "share orientations of the three main campus constituencies—students, faculty, and administrators—and that our organizational positions on the boundaries of these subsystems, our marginality, is our strength. Our uniqueness as student personnel workers rests on our ability to fashion significant educational environments, using the resources, values, norms, and opportunities of the variety of constituencies on our campuses. To the extent that we are successful in our innovative work, we will be respected, not because of position, but as a result of the impacts we have on campus life. Truly, student personnel workers have the opportunities to be central figures for campus improvement in an era when resources must be perceived as newly combined rather than as new." (p. 12).

Leadership is always expressed in groups or organizations, for it is a social function and the process by which a person helps a group or institution to meet its goals. Effective leadership balances large and small issues, respects those who differ, avoids compromising long-term objectives for short-term gains, and generates new strength and capability in the movement toward objectives. Effective leaders move in on situations, spell out issues, insist that problems be defined and solved, and possess energy for planning and reflection, for daily associations with people, for encounters with adversaries, for achieving agreements, and for accepting defeats in an environment of unrelenting pressure.

Some leadership functions may be carried out by administrators, others by faculty, administration, and students. Who does what is determined by what needs to be done and by who has the skills and time to do it.

When power is shared with skill and enthusiasm, everyone gains power, and no one loses. The group dynamics movement uses the term "synergy" to describe this phenomenon of synthesizing available group energy.

The call for visionary leadership challenges us to inspire confidence and a desire for constructive actions and to show the numerous constituencies a vision for their institution and human development that can match and overcome contemporary obstacles.

Postsecondary education is not mere research, exposure to professors, a discipline of study, or taking of examinations. It is not merely being oriented to an institution, selecting appropriate curricula, securing advice and counsel, attending lectures and concerts and athletic events, dreaming about the future, or laughing and joking with faculty, staff, and other students. It is not just learning anything, doing anything, or believing anything. It is not merely being satisfied or frustrated with processes, passing or failing examinations and courses, or experiencing joy and sadness. Postsecondary education is all of this and more. It is especially a movement toward thinking rationally, acting purposively, and dealing humanely with challenges.

We must challenge members of the educational community to stretch. We must confront each other with possibilities, reinforce positive strivings and responses, remove and minimize barriers, and celebrate successes. We must model the effective scholarly practitioner by giving attention to inquiry initiatives, interactions that make a difference, and to the joy of transcendence and synergizing. We must point to other methods and reinforce modeling. We must affirm the importance and value of each individual within the learning community and the significance of their contributions.

Our institutions of postsecondary education are capable of continuous change, renewal, and responsiveness. As concerned administrators, we must do more than manage change; we must be leaders of change. Visionary leadership makes things happen and fosters working together to facilitate change and improvement in the workplace. As the builders of tomorrow, the challenge is clear. We must reinforce movement toward the realization of our noble mission. We must inspire confidence, trust, and support for the fulfillment of a mission that requires synergisms far greater than the administration or the institution itself.

References

Cross, K. P. "Planning for the Future of the Student Personnel Profession." *Journal of College Student Personnel,* 1980a, *22* (2), 99–104.

Cross, K. P. "Two Scenarios for Higher Education's Future." *AAHE Bulletin,* 1980b, *33* (1), 1, 14–16.

Silverman, R. J. "The Student Personnel Administrator as Leading-Edge Leader." *NASPA Journal,* 1980, *18* (2), 10–15.

Milton E. Wilson is dean for Student Affairs and Professor of Counseling and Personnel Services Education at Kent State University.

This commentary has a dual focus: an analysis of the student voices presented in the main body of the book and an analysis of how student affairs professionals can use developmental theory as a guide for designing campus environments that may facilitate student development.

A Developmental Perspective on the Student Voice

L. Lee Knefelkamp

The primary purpose of this chapter is to discuss what college students of today are saying about their lives and their experience of the college or university environment through the metaphor of developmental theory. It is also important to comment on the importance and meaning of what DeCoster and Mable have done in their study: they have listened to students and through that process have legitimized the student voices. Their listening reflects three very important perspectives of our profession:

1. *A basic trust in students.* "I think that simple as it may seem, it is worth saying: a fundamental belief in students is more important than anything else. This fundamental belief is not a sentimental matter: it is a very demanding matter of realistically conceiving the student where he or she is, and at the same time never losing sight of where he or she can be" (Rich, 1979, pp. 66).

2. *A fundamental belief that student voices must be heard and empowered.* Rich (1979) recently commented about teaching writing at City College: "What has held me, and what I think holds many who teach basic writing, are the hidden veins of possibility running through students who don't know—and strongly doubt—that this is what they were born for, but who may find it out to their own amazement, students who, grim with self-deprecation and

D. A. DeCoster and P. Mable (Eds.), *New Directions for Student Services: Understanding Today's Students,* no. 16. San Francisco: Jossey Bass, 1981.

prophecies of their own failure or fight with a fear they cannot express, can be lured into sticking it out to some moment of breakthrough, when they discover that they have ideas that are valuable, even original, and can express those ideas on paper. What fascinates and gives hope in a time of slashed budgets, enlarging class size, and national depression is the possibility that many of these young men and women may be gaining the kind of critical perspective on their lives and the skill to bear witness that they have never before had in our country's history" (p. 67).

3. *A commitment to the role of the student affairs profession as one that includes the deliberate design of environments to facilitate development.* Perry (1970) discussed his own study in terms that apply here: "Finally, the study makes salient the courage required of the student in each step of development. This demand upon courage implies a reciprocal obligation for the educational community: to recognize the student's courage and to confirm the membership one achieves as one assumes the risks of each forward movement. This is a creative obligation: to find ways to encourage" (p. 215).

Students of all ages are courageously asking some very fundamental Eriksonian-type questions as we learned in the early chapters of this book: Who am I? What am I to believe and value and how am I to decide? Who and how am I to love? Adrienne Rich (#6, 1971, p. 58) writes of the experience of identity confusion ("moving through a bad light"), of finding someone there to listen ("you are beside me like a wall"), and of rejoicing in the dialogue—all the while knowing that the answers, if there are to be answers, must come from within ("your clarities may not reach me, but your attention will"). I read the chapters in this book, the student quotations, and the empathic analysis of the editors, and I want to say with Rich: "It is amazing that your eyes are to be met." It is amazing that these student voices have been heard, legitimized, and distilled for us all to hear.

Tom Hayden, who passionately cried out to be heard in the sixties, was asked when he spoke to the American College Personnel Association's (ACPA) national convention several years ago: "What do modern students need?" He replied: "The same things they've always needed—friends, role models, someone to hear what they have to say." Nevitt Sanford, whose profound intellect has given our profession powerful concepts, told the same body in 1981 that one of the most developmentally facilitating things college administrators, faculty, and student affairs professionals could do would be to interview students on a regular basis. All the while I am rejoicing in this study, this legitimizing of the student voice, I am reminded that listening is not enough, that empathy is necessary but not sufficient, that action must follow. Students are asking questions. And because we are listening, student affairs professionals have a special obligation in the

educational community to ask a series of parallel questions: How will we listen and interpret what we hear? How will we respond now that we have heard? How will we create developmentally facilitative environments in which students can as Erikson (1959) suggests:
- Experiment with roles
- Experience choices and decision making
- Experience meaningful achievement
- Live and work in an environment free from excessive anxiety
- Have time for reflection and introspection.

The chapters on student concerns are replete with issues that can be interpreted through the filter systems of our most respected theorists. Indeed, my own students are always teasing me that I often seem to find reality mirroring theory rather than the other way around. However, if developmental theory is useful in the analysis of characteristics of students, it is just as powerful a tool for the analysis of the characteristics of college environments—whether those environments are defined as entire schools, living facilities, the influence of peers, the atmosphere of a classroom or an advising session, family expectations, or the societal and institutional pressure to choose a major and a career. Nevitt Sanford emphasized three major themes in his 1981 speech to the ACPA: (1) that the purpose of higher education is the facilitation of mature personality development in students, (2) that such facilitation should be guided by appropriate personality theories, and (3) that educators should therefore use such theoretical knowledge in the creation of developmentally facilitating environments and experiences.

Developmental theories (such as those of Erikson, Perry, Chickering, Marcia, Loevinger, Kohlberg, Roy Heath, Douglas Heath, Cross, Levinson, Neugarten, White, Vaillant, and Gould) and person-environment theories (such as those of Holland, Clark and Trow, Pace and Stern, and Myers-Briggs) provide the practitioner with the ability to do the following tasks:

1. *Develop a concept of the mature personality.* Regardless of the terminology used, there is general agreement among developmental theorists of the characteristics of the mature person. Browning (1979) summarizes those qualities with reference to Erikson. He presents the mature personality as possessing the qualities of trust, autonomy initiative, industry, a sense of identity, a capacity for intimacy, the ability to be generative, and a sense of integrity. Such individuals are also characterized as having the "virtues" of hope, will, purpose, competence, fidelity, love, care, and wisdom. These qualities represent living, constantly developing goals. They are experienced, exercised at different times in different ways over the life span. And they are experienced in the context of the larger society and of the various communities to which the individual belongs, lives and works. "The maturity end goals described by each of the theories are remarkably similar to the end goals of higher education itself: the facilitation of human beings

who can reason as well as read; who possess insight as well as knowledge; who have the capacity for empathy and ethical conduct; who recognize, appreciate, and are not threatened by individual differences; and who have developed the interpersonal skills and thinking processes necessary for living in a complex and diverse society" (Knefelkamp, 1980, p. 18).

2. *Analyze the student voice in terms of appropriate theories.* The choice of theories used will depend on: the content concerns of the student, the developmental processes implied by the student, and the specific environmental context that the student is describing. Developmental and person/environment theories attempt to provide accurate, descriptive views of general student characteristics concerning identity issues, personality typology factors, cognitive ways of how the student is reasoning about and interpreting the issue or situation, and environmental influences. They are general descriptive models and are not directly prescriptive in nature.

3. *Translate those general student characteristics into accurate and more specific descriptions of student characteristics in the context of specific environments, roles, expectations.* This would involve examining such factors as: student-as-learner, student-as-peer, student-as-group member, student-as-career-chooser, and student-as-seeker of a firmer sense of self. For example, Perry helps us understand how students think about the learning process, while Chickering helps us understand the emotional sensitivity students have when facing a crisis of intellectual competency. Person/environment theory suggests that the press of the classroom environment can by analyzed with respect to those issues. Used in combination, these models provide an empathic view of how students' thoughts and feelings are likely to affect their classroom behavior and how the behavior of the instructor and design of the learning environment is likely to affect the student. This act of translation is prescriptive in nature and has implications for environmental design.

4. *Analyze the specific student characteristics in terms of Sanford's concepts of challenge and support.* This step demands the exercise of our feeling intellect to determine how student characteristics relate to issues of intellectual and emotional disequilibrium.

5. *Analyze the characteristics of the environment in which the student is living or working in terms of challenge and support.* Does the environment provide a sufficient balance of challenge and support to be facilitative? Is it neutral? Is it actually inhibiting? Are its characteristics antidevelopmental?

6. *Design an environment to match student developmental needs.* Such an environment allows the student to experiment, experience, reflect, and choose in an atmosphere free from excess anxiety; it emphasizes the mutual concepts of students as individuals and a people who live within the context of a community. I believe that this is the most prescriptive step and one that we must set as a high priority. Our profession should be the catalyst for helping college and university personnel to understand that they are critical

sources of role modeling of those qualities of trust, care, purpose, and hope—"hope that despite loneliness, students can make meaning in their lives; hope that despite the risks of uncertainty in nearly everything they encounter, they can dare to enter into relationships with loved ones; hope that the sense of individuality that has been so newly won is also compatible with a sense of community" (Knefelkamp, 1980, p. 22).

7. *Implement the developmentally designed program, experience, workshop classroom, discussion group.*

8. *Evaluate, redesign if necessary, terminate the program if not effective.* Thus the process of theory-to-practice is really one that begins with practice—with the pragmatic concerns and needs of students and the characteristics of the college environment. One moves from an analysis of a pragmatic concern to description in the context of theory to translation to prescription, and finally, to practice again (Rodgers and Widick, 1980; Wells and Knefelkamp, 1981). Within this context, I have selected from the chapters in the first half of this book several student concerns that seem to be salient and that lend themselves to this type of analysis.

Career Orientation and Academic Experience

The student voices in this book ask us to consider in particular, issues that arise around (1) career choices and (2) quality of learning. Have we organized our colleges in such a way as to add to the pressure that students feel to decide about a major and a career before they are ready to make those decisions? Is it possible for us to facilitate the choice of a major and at the same time legitimize the student who would be better served if there were more time for exploration, experimentation, and reflection? If it is true that students need a great deal of information before making a choice that will satisfy their complex needs, is it not also true that we must begin to educate faculty and staff about the complexities of the career process? We must find ways in which the choosing student can be comforted in the struggle and made to feel that there are opportunities both on campus and off campus that can be integrated into the academic experience that will facilitate self-exploration and decision making.

The students talk about fragmentation—about getting bits and pieces of information. They do not talk about living in a community in which they feel that the various parts of the community are working together to help them with this issue. I believe that most colleges and universities have all the "parts" (career centers, counseling centers, orientation offices, activities offices, faculty, advising centers, offices of experiential learning) but little integration and coordination. What is needed is an issue focus and a will to work together to provide an environment that is coherent and that fosters the ability of students to make contacts between and among all the various parts which compose the total learning experience. I would suggest that staff and faculty form working, programmatic task forces that can: (1) understand the issue, (2) seek practical methods of working in harmony, and (3) publicize a unified approach to students.

Have we inadvertently placed such an emphasis on credits and grades that we have contributed to the students' view that education is as much quantity of information as it is quality of thinking? I was impressed by how much the students craved meaningful contact with faculty, and how much they found that experience lacking. I felt a sense of irony as I read the student statements because I have spent the last several years of my professional life working closely with faculty who wish to improve the quality of the classroom, who are almost overwhelmed by the complexity of the teaching task and the diversity of students in the modern classroom, and who are freely, enthusiastically embracing the perspectives they gain through the study of student development theories that are relevant to classroom teaching, advising sessions, and general student life. Faculty care deeply about students, about teaching, and about the loss of the mutuality of a community of scholars. DeCoster and Mable found that the "most telling characteristics of meaningful faculty-student relationships is their scarcity." There is profound loneliness here. But it is not just student loneliness. Faculty are lonely as well—and feeling just as misunderstood.

I would suggest that one of the most important and necessary roles of our profession in the eighties is to: (1) help the students understand the learning process and (2) help faculty understand how students learn and how developmental theory can aid in the analysis of teaching in specific classrooms and of designing entire curricular sequences. We must take the initiative to form or support existing groups of faculty who are working on this issue. Perhaps never before in the history of the profession have we had such an opportunity to involve ourselves with the central academic core of the university environment. But our knowledge of students and theory is not sufficient. We must learn to know faculty and their characteristics as well as we know students. We must become partners in the search for improving and enhancing the teaching process. It is, I believe, an artistic process, similar to what Rich (1978, p. 7) calls "the true nature of poetry. The drive to connect. The dream of a common language." Both faculty and students want to connect—to make meaning together in the classroom and in the advising relationship. Perhaps student development theory is a source of a common language that will allow us to work more effectively with faculty in this most critical of all areas.

Interpersonal Relationships and Individual Differences

When I read the sections related to these issues I heard concern for the development of autonomy—but I did not hear a concern for being a more involved member of the community. I heard feelings of loneliness and fear of failure, of wanting to feel that someone understood, but I did not hear that students were truly comfortable with others who were different from themselves. And yet the analysis also revealed that "they search for strength and humor and hope, and they wonder about society." Browning (1975) writes about the capacity for generativity, for caring, for seeing oneself as part of a community, for seeing oneself as part of a living link between the past and the future, for understanding and then responding to the nature of that which is to be cared for. He also writes about the general nongenerative nature of our modern society—a perspective echoed by Levine (1980), who analyzes the "meism" of the modern college student.

I would suggest that student affairs professionals have a critical role to play in this area. If we find students having difficulty with racial, religious, or life-style differences, then we must work cooperatively to do the following: (1) seek to provide forums for informal discussion about such issues; (2) take advantage of the opportunities to discuss when such issues arise naturally on the campus or in the news; (3) model behavior and thinking that allows individual differences to exist without necessarily approving of all behaviors, that distinguishes between evaluating issues or conduct and respecting individual beliefs and values; (4) seek to model the fact that involvement and activism are not synonomous with marching and protesting—but in fact involve much work, overtime; (5) seek to provide opportunities for cross-generational contact; and (6) provide frank and provocative discussions about ethical issues on the campus such as recruitment and retention, student consumerism, and academic dishonesty.

I believe that our profession may need to be a reasoned but raised voice on the campus calling these issues into public dialogue that involves students and administrators and staff. Students will, as any citizen will, conform to the norms of the community. If we have concerns about students in these important areas, then we must also look to ourselves and the modeling that the academic community collectively presents. If we want our students to be hopeful, then we must model hope. If we want them to be involved, then we must infect them with our own enthusiasm. If we want them to be compassionate, then we must help them learn to be empathic. If we want them to be less lonely, then perhaps we can find ways to encourage them to find each other and to find us. Given the pressures they face, perhaps it is we who should do the seeking. If there is too much silence among the various members of the academic community, then perhaps we can catalyze the search to find each other again and to legitimize each others' voices.

Summary

In the final analysis, theory is an empathic tool, one that helps us listen more carefully for issues and how students make meaning. The use of theory can be powerful for as Erica Jong (1973, p. 172) has written: "the most profound revolutions will come from the development of our capacity for empathy." In the end, we return to where we began: the simple, complex task of listening to students. That's where theory began to grow from the concrete analysis of our practices and the characteristics of ourselves, our students, and our environments to a theoretical understanding to a more informed and deliberate practice of the art of our profession.

References

Browning, D. S. *Generative Man.* New York: Dell, 1975.
Erikson, E. H. *Identity and the Life Cycle.* Psychological Issues Monograph, Vol. 1. new York: International Universities Press, 1959.
Jong, E. "Visionary Anger." In B. Gelpi, and A. Gelpi (Eds.), *Adrienne Rich's Poetry.* New York: Norton, 1975.
Knefelkamp, L. L. "Faculty and Student Development in the '80s: Renewing the Community of Scholars." *Current Issues in Higher Education*, No. 5. Washington D. C.: American Association for Higher Education, 1980.
Levine, A. *When Dreams and Heroes Died: A Portrait of Today's College Student.* San Francisco: Jossey-Bass, 1980.
Perry, W. G., Jr. *Forms of Intellectual and Ethical Development in the College Years: A Scheme.* New York: Holt, Rinehart and Winston, 1970.
Rich, A. *The Will to Change.* New York: Norton, 1971.
Rich, A. *The Dream of a Common Language.* New York: Norton, 1978.
Rich, A. *On Lies, Secrets, and Silence.* New York: Norton, 1979.
Rodgers, R., and Widick, C. "Theory to Practice: Uniting Concepts, Logic, and Creativity." In F. Newton, and K. Ender (Eds.), *Student Development Practices.* Springfield, Ill.: Thomas, 1980.
Wells, E., and Knefelkamp, L. L. "A Process Model of Practice-to-Theory-to-Practice." Model presented at Southeastern Association of College and University Housing Officers Regional Conference, Williamsburg, Va., February, 1981.

L. Knefelkamp is an Associate Professor of Counseling and Personnel Services at the University of Maryland. She also holds the position of Faculty Associate for Student Development in the Division of Student Affairs. Her work has its focus in the use of developmental theory in the design of learning environments and student personnel programs.

After integrating the messages from students with the wisdom of expert commentaries, the editors postulate future change strategies within four broad areas of reform.

Postsecondary Education Futures: Implications, Innovations, and Initiatives

*Phyllis Mable
David A. DeCoster*

While maintaining and even propagating the ideals of liberal education, college administrators, faculty, and students are responsible for the human development themes that unify postsecondary education. It should not be a matter of debate about the relative virtues of a particular program, but of analyzing our ability to humanize the educational experience and to purport the objective of total human development as the institutional commitment. Colleges and universities have a chance to put behind them the impersonality of the past years. Students, although sometimes hesitant to seek help, are eager for a more personalized approach to the problems facing them and to their educational pursuits.

Educators should not be nostalgic for a lost, largely illusory and certainly irretrievable time when "subjects" rather than "students" prevailed. The more worthy dream is one of optimism and can-do faith in students. Discovering that the success of postsecondary education is not necessarily embedded in cognitive knowledge may be a rather painful insight for some faculty and administrators. Educators, nonetheless, must start experimenting with student-oriented approaches to collegiate life that prepare graduates for the world of citizens and workers within the expansiveness of social change. This venture could liberate the personal creativity and drive that will make American education blossom and prosper.

Education will be better only when administrators, faculty, and students are convinced that it is up to them to think, take risks, and make it better. The following requisites represent a new departure—an awakening to rescue the future of postsecondary education from a descending path of impersonalization and self-indulgence. These requisites expound specific implications, innovations, and initiatives; shape human lives through student-oriented approaches; and recognize the value of caring, compassion, interdependence, integrity, ethics, and excellence.

Reforming Management Approaches

Needed: Major changes in educational practices in an inhumane educational system

1. *Initiate needs assessment studies to provide data for making informed program decisions.* Educators and students conducting needs assessment must understand the problem areas being assessed, be clear about the tasks, and know how the results will be utilized. Responsiveness to students' problems can be improved as there is a systematic method of collecting data used to make program decisions relevant to problems, students, and societal realities.

2. *Incorporate human development courses and opportunities to actively assist students who struggle with such recurrent themes as career, interpersonal relationships, social responsibility, life skills, and future directions.* The goals would be personal development through increased self-understanding; exploration of personal insight; development of purpose and expansion of caring; integration of identity, values, and personal commitments; discovery of self; and clarification of new ideas, perspectives, and interests.

3. *Insist on a comprehensive program of student services, defined as a set of standard requirements essential to support the totality of student life on campus and to provide a secure, yet stimulating, community environment.* It is imperative to deliver basic services with maximum efficiency and minimal hassle in order to avoid dissatisfaction with the academic and social life of the institution as it relates to students' rights and responsibilities. Student services that function consistently contribute to student retention and support, avoid personal disappointments and setbacks, and enhance motivation and performance.

4. *Engage in the study of developmental theory to know students' needs and patterns of growth and change and to understand the psychological development of students, as well as their motivations, styles of learning, and potential learning difficulties.* Increased knowledge of theory requires educators to focus on a

different form of expectation—not what is expected from subject matter in the way of learning, but what is expected from students with their unique individual differences. The student development dimension must be incorporated in the humanistic approach to educating the "whole person" and enhancing student skills and competencies that contribute to lifelong learning and growth.

5. *Design a plan for evaluating programs and services to ensure quality, adequacy, and effectiveness in meeting student needs and expectations.* Levels of program evaluation that are based on practical and developmental benefits to students and are appropriate to individual differences will be vital to helping students identify and achieve their educational goals. The years ahead will offer opportunities as well as risks as institutions strive to develop programs and services that are more meaningful, humane, and constructive.

Resolving Learning Responsibility

Needed: Student awareness and a new sense of involvement and responsibility.

1. *Encourage student participation in residence education learning experiences to promote individual identity, the spirit of citizenship and community, and interpersonal and motivational skills.* Residence education leaders must utilize their close relationships with students to help them understand how thoroughly residential learning contributes to satisfaction with the collegiate experience, to clarification of present and future career and life-style decisions, and to recognition of self-worth and determination that requires self-understanding and skill in relating easily to others.

2. *Institute real mechanisms for student inclusion, energy, and contribution in campus governance to advance collaborative, creative decision making that generates excitement among students for their education.* Student involvement in campus governance must give all students a much greater and detailed description of what they are supposedly entitled to—and educators should honestly provide an immediate basis for comparisons, questions, and procedures. This charge includes clearly stated institutional expectations regarding academic requirements and integrity so that the current cloud of unhealthy and dishonest academic competition can be dissipated. While students have achieved some control over their autonomy, their activities, and their interests, they are less involved in course, institution, and consumer planning. Students, who strive to be heard and who are allowed to provide themselves and their peers with quality education, want to serve society's occupational structure with people who perform well and who will continue their education after graduation.

3. *Advocate student involvement on campus to encourage student retention and growth through significant investments of time in their own educational pursuits.* The

profound diversity brought to college campuses by increasing numbers of women, minorities, adult learners, and part-time students, sometimes works in subtle ways. The spirit and tone of the small town community must be preserved while we eradicate big-city anonymity. Involvement requires educators who advocate learning experiences that involve students in individual responsibility for themselves and for the communities around them in the classroom, residence halls, fraternities and sororities, and campus activity programs.

4. *Determine a way to recognize student involvement in extracurricular experiences so that students can evaluate their programs, understand skills and competencies gained, design new opportunities and experiences for growth, and market themselves to prospective employers who seek leadership and interpersonal skills as well as academic learning.* What is basically needed is an educational record or transcript that completely describes student development.

Reclaiming the Value of Teaching

Needed: A consistent plan for student-faculty relations and a coalition between faculty and student affairs educators.

1. *Establish teaching and learning relationships to improve the quality of academic advising and to begin programs that aid students in assessing their current individual development, setting goals for accomplishment, determining learning experiences, evaluating progress, and recording results.* Students must be involved in their own education, and faculty and administrators must become colleagues, mentors, counselors, and advisors, as well as teachers and researchers. These are tasks not easily fulfilled, but there can be no commitment to human development unless pressure is exerted to ensure a new atmosphere with teachers who care about students and who believe in exchanging aspirations, hopes, and concerns.

2. *Enable and encourage faculty and students to think anew about themselves and society as it is and as it is becoming.* Faculty must help to combine an honest concern with self with the equally legitimate concern with knowledge and community. Education is the foundation of a workable democracy that supports dedication, compassion, justice, and every individual's chance and expectation for learning. Students must be prepared for life and community responsibilities. The classroom experience must help students to train their intelligence, acquire and apply the information of academic disciplines, and understand the twenty-first century families, citizens, and workers.

3. *Build coalitions between academic and student affairs educators to help turn institutions toward a future where all people will be encouraged to achieve an education commensurate with their capacities.* If the goals of postsecondary education are concerned with the development of the full potentialities of human beings

and society, their academic affairs and student affairs must agree on a total program of curricular and extracurricular experiences that influence future cultural and social systems. Administrators, faculty, and students need to begin collaborating about what priorities postsecondary education should address in the coming years.

Refreshing the Collegiate Environment

Needed: Support for student consumer rights, educational equity, and personal beliefs or ideals.

1. *Change teaching and learning environments to accommodate older students, women, minorities, and part-time students—not by forced circumstances but by recognized opportunities.* For educators to ignore the learning society as it exists is both cautious and curious. The value of knowing what kinds of populations will be served and what kinds of experiences they desire calls for strong ties with these students who have new stakes in the educational future. Diverse student populations are going to advertise, specify, and get what they want. Above all, institutions must realize that students view a college education as a right of citizenship and not a privilege for the elite. A keen awareness among educators of the purpose of education is necessary to identify and meet student needs, to cement liberal education and preparation for employment, and to nurture self-development in a context of concern for society.

2. *Expand student services and developmental programs to build a collaborative student and university community by greater involvement of students as paraprofessionals, peer counselors, advisors, and collegial leaders.* This cadre of alert and aware students can rouse other students to come to grips with ethical, moral, governance, community, and social issues. Thus, students will be the active influencers of their own education, the integrators of students into the institutional work setting, the expanders of services and programs relevant to collegiate life, and the providers of a host of real-world learning experiences.

3. *Help student consumers address their individual needs to realize their roles as forecasters of the commodity education.* Institutions must recognize the potential of today's campus movements—foreign policy, minority student survival, urban problems, cuts in student financial aid, campus governance—and educate students and their leaders on how important it is to support both grass-roots organizing and student government activity. On campus, student activists will concern themselves with the quality of teaching and governance, with services provided for students by students—bookstore, daycare, food cooperatives, peer counseling, family planning—with tuition costs and student fees. Students are weary of education that is inhumane,

undemocratic, and unresponsive. Not the least of such issues is that students feel entitled to the undisputed right to tax themselves and utilize student fee monies to resolve campus deficiencies.

4. *Admit to the issues of minority student survival and race relations to define the concerns and fully utilize the fragments of social integration as they are achieved daily.* Administrators, faculty, and students must address openly and deeply the rights, problems, and opportunities of minorities and to realize the tremendous importance for cross-cultural and social understanding that have not yet been achieved within the typical campus community.

Summary

Not in a long while has so much knowledge about students led to so much opportunity for allowing institutions to expend time and energy "brainstorming" about the future. The rewards for students, and perhaps the worry for postsecondary institutions, is that the arsenal of knowledge will focus the future on human existence required to prepare students for community participation and leadership. The Carnegie Council on Policy Studies in Higher Education reports in a dramatic way that half of the college student populations by the twenty-first century will be different from those enrolled in 1960. There will be more women than men, a balance of students over and under twenty-one years of age, about equal numbers of part-time and full-time students, and about one minority student in every four of the college population. Requisites for postsecondary futures will require lifelong learning experiences for educators as well as students, particularly as the new student consumer becomes the market related to society's needs. Students will transform campuses into a mosaic of experiences connecting education to life. They are communicating a message that is both a warning and a challenge. For educators, understanding today's students becomes a matter of first priority—followed by determined action and the courage to change.

Part Three
Appendixes

Appendix A

Participating Institutions and Campus Coordinators

College Student Life Project
1977-1981

(N = 28)

Institution	Coordinator
Appalachian State University (North Carolina)	David McIntire
Auburn University (Alabama)	Charles Schroeder
Buena-Vista College (Iowa)	Donna Hunter
Cumberland County Community College (New Jersey)	Gretchen Naff
Georgia Southwestern	Kemper Smith
Germanna Community College (Virginia)	Richard Ridge
Indiana University	Joyce Martello
John Tyler Community College (Virginia)	Gretchen Naff
Lewis and Clark State College (Idaho)	David Cox
Marquette University (Wisconsin)	George Shoffner
Millikin University (Illinois)	Greg Jones
North Carolina State University at Raleigh	Sue Moore
Ohio University	Sandy Hereth
Oklahoma State University	Kent Sampson
Radford College (Virginia)	Craig Ullom
Regis College (Colorado)	Terry Soley
Southwest Minnesota State University	Robert Krause
University of Connecticut	Jane Fried
University of Florida	Margaret Beistle
University of Georgia	Kathy Rennell
University of Michigan	Leroy Williams
University of Missouri at Rolla	Paul Rifkin
University of Nebraska at Lincoln	Dolores Simpson-Kirkland
University of Rhode Island	Maryanne Cunningham
University of Vermont	Keith Miser
University of Wisconsin-Stevens Point	Fred Leafgren
Virginia Commonwealth University	Phyllis Mable
West Virginia Institute of Technology	Linda Olesen

Appendix B

Profile of Characteristics for Student Participants

College Student Life Project
1977-1981

(N = 617)

College Classification	Percent
Freshman	29.7
Sophomore	27.7
Junior	21.2
Senior	20.6
Graduate	2.6
Other	1.2

Sex	Percent
Female	50.9
Male	49.1

Age	Percent
17	1.2
18	18.8
19	21.4
20	19.1
21	17.0
22	6.7
23	2.9
24	2.7
25 or older	10.3

Religious Preference	Percent
Jewish	2.9
Protestant	40.5
Roman Catholic	30.2
Other	4.7
No Preference	14.7
No Response	7.0

Marital Status	Percent
Single	89.6
Married	6.5
Divorced	1.2
Other	1.5
No Response	1.2

Racial-Ethnic Background	Percent
Black	11.4
Hispanic	1.9
White	83.0
American Indian	0.6
American Oriental	0.3
Foreign Citizen	0.6
Other	0.9
No Response	1.4

Residence	Percent
With Parents	5.8
Off-Campus Housing	16.6
Residence Hall	60.7
Sorority or Fraternity	10.4
Other	5.5

Type of Institution	Percent
Public, 4 year	70.1
Public, 2 year	9.7
Private, 4 year, denominational	20.2

Major Field of Study	Percent
Arts and Humanities	12.9
Biological Sciences	7.0
Business	17.4
Education	13.9
Engineering	10.5
Physical Sciences	1.4
Professional	7.7
Social Science	16.7
Undecided	8.0
Other	4.5

Career Choice	Percent
Accountant	4.4
Artist	1.1
Business	7.4
Clergy	1.4
Counselor	3.7
Dentist	1.5
Engineer	5.9
Farmer	0.4
Foreign Service	0.6
Health Professions	0.4
Journalist	3.0
Law Officer	1.1
Lawyer	8.5
Military	0.7
Nurse	2.6
Physician	3.0
Psychologist	1.5
Skilled Trades	0.7
Social Work	3.7
Teacher	16.2
Therapist	5.2
Veterinarian	0.4
Other	1.9
Unknown	24.7

Index

A

Academic experiences and career orientations, 7–14; and career choices, 12–14; and motives for seeking a college education, 7–9; and the quality of academic experience, 9–12
Academic honesty, 72. *See also* Personal values and behavior of college students
Academic pressure, coping with. *See* Personal values and behavior of college students
Activists, student. *See* Student activists, a new breed of
Administrative leadership on college campuses, 89–98; and administrative and managerial implications, 91–95; and educational goals and objectives, 94–95; facilitating student development by means of, 89, 93–94; and the need for visionary leadership, 95–97; and research and evaluation, 92–93; and student personnel administrators, 96; and students' educational experiences, 90–91
Administrative power on college campuses. *See* Administrative leadership on college campuses; Student apathy and self-interest
Advisors, college, attitudes of college students toward, 12, 44–45, 47, 72
Alcohol usage among college students. *See* Personal values and behavior of college students
American College Personnel Association (ACPA), 100, 101
Apathy, student. *See* College environment, the; Social and political issues, student attitudes toward; Student apathy and self-interest
Association of Governing Boards of Colleges and Universities (AGB), 80–81
Athletes, college, and academic honesty. *See* Academic honesty
Autonomy, development of, by college students, 104–105. *See also* Growing up, the pains of, for college students

B

Black students. *See* Minorities, attitudes of college students toward
Boards of regents, college, 80
Boards of trustees, college, 80
Browning, D. S., 101, 105
Budget cuts of President Reagan, 81

C

Campus Crusade, 55
Career choices, decisions regarding. *See* Academic experience and career orientations; Developmental theories as guides for promoting student development; Student apathy and self-interest
Career planning. *See* Career choices, decisions regarding
Carnegie Council on Policy Studies in Higher Education, 112
Carnegie Foundation for the Advancement of Teaching, 79
Change Magazine, 79–80
Cheating on college campuses. *See* Academic honesty
Chickering, A. W., 101, 102
Chronicle of Higher Education, The, 81, 85
City College, 99
Civil Rights Act, 61
College education, motives for seeking. *See* Academic experiences and career orientations
College environment, the, 12, 15–22, 72, 111–112; and extracurricular involvement, 21–22; and the importance of community involvement, 15; and institutional decision making, 18–20; and involvement in student governance, 18–20; and leisure time, 20–22; and the living environment, 15–18

121

College environments, designing, to support student development. *See* Developmental theories as guides for promoting student development; Future of postsecondary education
Collegiate friendships. *See* College environment, the; Peer relationships, influence of
Commonwealth Association of Students, 87n
Community involvement, importance of, to campus life. *See* College environment, the
Commuting students, 38–39, 74
Cost, rising, of a college education, 63–64
Cross, K. P., 93, 96, 101

D

DeCoster, D. A., 1–3, 7–47, 49–66, 77, 86, 99, 104, 107–112
Developmental theories as guides for promoting student development, 99–106; and career orientation and academic experience, 103–104; and choosing the appropriate theory, 102; and the concept of the mature personality, 101–102; and descriptions of general student characteristics, 102; and the design of an appropriate environment, 102–103; and interpersonal relationships and individual differences, 104–105; and the quality of learning, 103–104
Dishonesty on college campuses. *See* Academic honesty
Dormitory life. *See* College environment, the; Growing up, the pains of, for college students
Downey, K., 2, 77–87
Drug usage among college students. *See* Personal values and behavior of college students

E

Education, practical, vs. philosophical education. *See* Academic experiences and career orientations
Employment opportunities, effect of college education on. *See* Academic experiences and career orientations
Erikson, E. H., 100, 101
Ethical issues relating to college life. *See* Personal values and behavior of college students
Extracurricular activities. *See* College environment, the

F

Faculty members, relationships of students with. *See* Interpersonal relationships of college students; Professors, attitudes of students toward
Families, relationships of college students with their. *See* Growing up, the pains of, for college students; Interpersonal relationships of college students
Financial motivations of students. *See* Academic experiences and career orientations; Personal development, student concern with
Fraternity and sorority living. *See* College environment, the
Friendship patterns among college students. *See* Interpersonal relationships of college students; Peer relationships, influence of
Future of postsecondary education, 107–112; and accommodation of special students groups, 111–112; and a coalition between faculty and student affairs educators, 110–111; and needed changes in educational practices, 108–109; and needed student involvement, 109–110; and needed support for student consumer rights and educational equity, 111–112; and reclaiming the value of teaching, 110–111; and reforming management approaches, 108–109; and refreshing the collegiate environment, 111–112; and resolving learning responsibility, 109–110; and student-faculty relations, 110

G

Gay students. *See* Minorities, attitudes of college students toward
Goal setting in college, 12

Growing up, the pains of, for college students, 69–76; and peers and studying in dormitories, 70–72; and prejudice, 71–72; and the responsibilities of students, 74–76; and the role of faculty members, 72–74; and separation from family and home, 69–70; and sexual freedom, 71

H

Hayden, T., 100
Heath, D., 101
Heath, R. 101
Homesickness of college students. *See* Interpersonal relationships of college students
Homosexual students. *See* Minorities, attitudes of college students toward
Humanizing the educational experience, 107–109

I

Identity problems of students, 17
Institutional decision making, student participation in. *See* College environment, the
Interpersonal relationships of college students, 35–47; and the effect of commuting, 38–39; and homesickness and loneliness, 35–37; and peer relationships, 35–40, 46; and relationships with faculty members, 42–46, 47; and relationships with parents, 40–42, 46
Involvement, student. *See* College environment, the; Apathy, student

J

Jacobson, R. L., 81
Job advancement. *See* Career planning
Jong, E., 106

K

Katz, J., 2, 69–76
Kennedy, J. F., 78
Kennedy, R. F., 78
Kent State University, 2, 98n

King, M. L., Jr., 78
Knefelkamp, L. L., 2, 99–106
Ku Klux Klan, 52

L

Learning process, helping students understand, 104
Learning, quality of, 103–104
Leisure time on campus. *See* College environment, the
Levine, A., 79, 86, 105
Lifelong learning, 21, 65
Life-styles, collegiate. *See* College environment, the; Growing up, the pains of, for college students; Personal values and behavior of college students
Living conditions on campus. *See* College environment, the; Growing up, the pains of, for college students

M

Mable, P., 1–3, 7–47, 49–66, 77, 86, 99, 104, 107–112
Marijuana usage among college students. *See* Personal values and behavior of college students
Maturation process, the, in college students. *See* Growing up, the pains of, for college students
Minorities, attitudes of college students toward, 49–56, 71–72, 111–112; and black students, 50–53; and gay students, 53–54; and Hispanic students, 52, 55; and Native American students, 53, 55; and religious groups, 55; and women, 54–55
Monetary motives of students. *See* Academic experiences and career orientations; Financial motivations of students

N

Nader, R., 79–80
National Student Association (NSA), 84
National Student Educational Fund (NSEF), 2, 84, 86, 87n
National Student Lobby (NSL), 84

O

Older students on campus, 21–22, 111

P

Parental influences on college students. *See* Interpersonal relationships of college students; Personal values and behavior of college students
Part-time work at college. *See* College environment, the
Peer relationships, influence of, on college students. *See* Growing up, the pains of, for college students; Interpersonal relationships of college students; Personal values and behavior of college students
Perry, W. G., Jr., 75, 100, 101, 102
Personal development, student concern with. *See* Social and political issues, student attitudes toward; Student apathy and self-interest
Personal values and behavior of college students, 23–34; and academic honesty, 30–34; and academic pressures, 25; and alcohol usage, 24–27, 34; and drug usage, 24–27, 34; and influences of family on, 23, 34; and influence of peer relationships on, 23, 27, 34; and influence of religious beliefs on, 23–24, 34; and sexual relationships, 27–30, 34
Person-environment theories, 101
Piaget, J., 75
Pluralistic campus environment. *See* Minorities, attitudes of college students toward
Political issues, attitudes of students toward. *See* Social and political issues, student attitudes toward
Professors, attitudes of students toward, 11–12, 42–46, 72. *See also* Growing up, the pains of, for college students; Interpersonal relationships of college students

R

Racial attitudes among college students *See* Minorities, attitudes of college students toward
Reagan, R. 81
Reforming postsecondary education. *See* Future of postsecondary education
Religious influences on college students. *See* Personal values and behavior of college students
Residence hall advisors, 46
Residence halls. *See* College environment, the
Rich, A., 99–100, 104
Rodgers, R., 103

S

Sanford, N., 100, 101, 102
Self-disciplines, need of, for success in college, 11
Sexual relationships on college campuses. *See* Growing up, the pains of, for college students; Personal values and behavior of college students
SGA. *See* Student government associations
Silverman, R. J., 96
Social and political issues, student attitudes toward, 57–66; and career planning, 64; and changes in social concerns, 60–62; and competition for grades, 64; and financial motivations, 57; and the mood of today's college students, 63–65; and personal development, 58–60; and reactions to political issues, 62–63; and student apathy, 62–63
State student associations (SSAs), 84–87. *See also* Student apathy and self-interest
State University of New York at Stony Brook, 2, 76n
Stern, 101
Student activists, a new breed of. *See* Student apathy and self-interest; Future of postsecondary education

Student affairs educators, 73–74, 105, 110–111
Student apathy. *See* Apathy, student
Student apathy and self-interest, 77–87; and the concentration of administrative power, 80–82; and conditions perpetuating student apathy, 79–80; and factors contributing to social and political apathy, 78–79; and state and national student associations, 84–87; and student activities offices, 81; and student governing bodies, 82–84
Student development, facilitating. *See* Developmental theories as guides for promoting student development; Humanizing the educational experience
Student expectations of college. *See* Academic experiences and career orientations
Student governance. *See* College environment, the; Student apathy and self-interest
Student government. *See* Student governance
Student government associations (SGA), 82–83, *See also* Student governance

Study habits of college students, 70–72

U

United States Student Association (USSA), 84, 86
University of Maryland, 2, 106n
University of Massachusetts at Amherst, 83
University of Nebraska, 3n

V

Veterans, motives of, in college, 14
Vietnam War, 78–79
Virginia Commonwealth University, 3n

W

Watergate scandal, 78–79
Wells, E., 103
West Chester State College, 87n
When Dreams and Heroes Died, 79
Widick, C., 103
Wilson, M. E., 2, 89–98
Women, motives of, in college, 14

STATEMENT OF OWNERSHIP, MANAGEMENT, AND CIRCULATION
(Required by 39 U.S.C. 3685)

1. Title of Publication: New Directions for Student Services. A. Publication number: USPS 449-070. 2. Date of filing: September 30, 1981. 3. Frequency of issue: quarterly. A. Number of issues published annually: four. B. Annual subscription price: $30 institutions; $18 individuals. 4. Location of known office of publication: 433 California Street, San Francisco (San Francisco County), California 94104. 5. Location of the headquarters or general business offices of the publishers: 433 California Street, San Francisco (San Francisco County), California 94104. 6. Names and addresses of publisher, editor, and managing editor: publisher—Jossey-Bass Inc., Publishers, 433 California Street, San Francisco, California 94104; editor—Ursula Delworth, Gary R. Hanson, University of Iowa, Counseling Center, Iowa City, Iowa 52242; managing editor—JB Lon Hefferlin, 433 California Street, San Francisco, California 94104. 7. Owner: Jossey-Bass Inc., Publishers, 433 California Street, San Francisco, California 94104. 8. Known bondholders, mortgages, and other security holders owning or holding 1 percent or more of total amount of bonds, mortgages, or other securities: same as No. 7. 10. Extent and nature of circulation: (Note: first number indicates the average number of copies of each issue during the preceding twelve months; the second number indicates the actual number of copies published nearest to filing date.) A. Total number of copies printed (net press run): 2529, 2521. B. Paid circulation, 1) Sales through dealers and carriers, street vendors, and counter sales: 85, 40. 2) Mail subscriptions: 874, 752. C. Total paid circulation: 959, 792. D. Free distribution by mail, carrier, or other means (samples, complimentary, and other free copies): 125, 125. E. Total distribution (sum of C and D): 1084, 917. F. Copies not distributed, 1) Office use, left over, unaccounted, spoiled after printing: 1455, 1604. 2) Returns from news agents: 0, 0. G. Total (sum of E, F1, and 2—should equal net press run shown in A): 2529, 2521.

I certify that the statements made by me above are correct and complete.

JOHN R. WARD
Vice-President